GRAMMAR

BOOHER'S RULES
OF
BUSINESS
GRAMMAR

101 Fast and Easy Ways
to Correct the
Most Common Errors

Dianna Booher

New York Chicago San Francisco Lisbon London
Madrid Mexico City Milan New Delhi
San Juan Seoul Singapore Sydney Toronto

1 2 3 4 5 6 7 8 9 0   DOC/DOC   0 1 0 9 8

ISBN: 978-0-07-148668-2
MHID: 0-07-148668-2

This publication is designed to provide accurate and authoritative information in regard to the subject matter covered. It is sold with the understanding that the publisher is not engaged in rendering legal, accounting, or other professional service. If legal advice or other expert assistance is required, the services of a competent professional person should be sought.

—*From a declaration of principles jointly adopted by a committee of the American Bar Association and a committee of publishers.*

McGraw-Hill books are available at special quantity discounts to use as premiums and sales promotions, or for use in corporate training programs. To contact a representative please visit the Contact Us pages at www.mhprofessional.com.

Contents

PART 2: PESKY PRONOUNS:
THE UNDERSTUDIES 55

Acknowledgments

My thanks to the following people for their help:

- ▶ Clients and attendees of writing and grammar workshops for their examples and lively discussions!
- ▶ The team at McGraw-Hill; Donya Dickerson, my editor; and Doris Michaels, my agent.
- ▶ Polly Fuhrman, for reading the manuscript and offering comments.
- ▶ Kari Gates, for reading the manuscript, offering comments, and helping to prepare the manuscript.
- ▶ The Booher team for picking up the slack in my absence from the office while I wrote yet another book!

DIANNA BOOHER

Introduction

No Louding

While visiting a museum in Beijing, I saw a sign that read "NO LOUD-ING." After a chuckle at what was obviously intended to mean "No Yelling" in this dignified place of artifacts and learning, I thought to myself: even if English is a second language here, you'd think that the curator would have verified the translation before posting signs everywhere.

But on later reflection, I've come to believe that people don't ask about things they don't know they don't know. That is, professionals today in every country and in every walk of life—professors, plumbers, engineers, accountants, salespeople, systems analysts, CEOs, and surveyors—make many of the same mistakes when they write and speak.

Some very smart people have difficulty with grammar. The peculiar thing is that they think other people don't notice! Imagine.

That's like an amateur carpenter saying to a master builder, "I'm making my granddaughter a desk chair for her dorm. One leg is an inch shorter than the other three. But I don't think that'll be noticeable, do you?" That's like a shipper saying to the accountant, "Our invoices don't agree with the bank statements, but I don't think that should create any questions." Or how far do you think a lawyer could get in court by inserting all the wrong dates in his client's sworn testimony and appeals?

We notice errors and imprecision in our own area of expertise—yet we think accuracy and precision in language don't matter. But they do.

For starters, grammar errors create clarity problems. Consider this sentence: "The 90-day clause in the contract, which is still pending approval, does not allow a price increase." If the contract is still pending approval, fine—that's what the sentence says. But if it's the 90-day clause that's pending approval, this is a problem waiting to happen. If the 90-day clause is pending approval, the sentence should read, "The contract's 90-day clause, which is still pending approval, does not allow a price increase."

A second reason to be concerned: coworkers and customers may not be amused by mistakes. In fact, they may become downright annoyed. Airline executives have discovered that dirty meal trays indicate to passengers that the mechanics don't service the engines. Similarly, poor grammar on the part of bank tellers suggests to customers that their home mortgages contain amortization errors. Perception overpowers logic in such cases.

Image counts.

To the listening ear of a client or a boss, bad grammar sounds like fingernails dragging across a chalkboard.

Yet bad grammar is like bad breath—even your best friends won't tell you. Besides, it's bad manners to go around embarrassing other people by pointing out their errors. After all, I don't want you to come over to my house and point out the cobwebs in the corners. So let's just do this little self-improvement project anonymously. (You can send a maid to my house any time by arrangement, thank you very much.)

But back to the topic of bad breath and bad grammar: If even your best buddies won't bring up the subject, that means you're responsible for finding out what you don't know and what can hurt you badly. You can't depend on your ear alone. What is often thought to be "bad grammar" may be fine. No rules broken. And what may sound like proper grammar to you simply because you've heard the usage often may actually be bad grammar.

In a nutshell, bad grammar can limit your social standing and stall your career. Let me explain in the words of a client, a CEO of a Fortune 500 company and a client of our communication training firm, talking about one of his vice presidents about to be dismissed.

"Roger has to go. He's just not the type we need around here. At the next rung of the ladder, these vice presidents will need to spend 90 percent of their time networking to bring in the big clients. They attend social functions, serve on community boards, entertain our biggest clients and their spouses for a week on a yacht in the Caribbean. Roger just doesn't have what it takes at this level. His hair looks disheveled half the time, and his grammar grates on me. In fact, his wife is an embarrassment socially when she accompanies him to client functions because her grammar is even worse than his. They're both college educated, . . . but he's just not polished."

Roger lost his job—not because of his technical skills, but because he refused to understand how much his language affected others' perceptions of his capabilities and of him personally.

Can you imagine reporting to the manager who sent out the following e-mail?

Hi Team;

Just a quick up date. Wanted to let you know that the supplier, which we had chosen for the Universal project has declined to accept our contract terms. And the fact that we will be conducting another round of meetings to agree on a alternative vendor by the end of June. On another note you're list of equipment, should be forwarded to me by May 5 however we may postpone budget discussions at the next staff meeting I'll let you know by Tuesday.

Regards,

Spike

It's embarrassing—like being unaware of the glob of mustard dribbled down the lapel of your suit as you stand up to deliver a presentation. Proper grammar is power. Pure and simple. Here's the rewrite:

Hi, Team,

Just a quick update: I wanted to let you know that the supplier we had chosen for the Universal project has declined to accept our contract terms. That means we will be conducting another round of meetings to agree on another vendor by the end of June.

On another note: Your list of equipment should be forwarded to me by May 5. However, we may postpone budget discussions at the next staff meeting; I'll let you know by Tuesday.

Regards,

Horatio

The importance of language to career and social standing is, with few exceptions, a universal issue. As I start to write this book, I'm on a speaking tour in Kuwait. In my audience are Kuwaitis, Iraqis, Egyptians, Swedes, Brits, Filipinos, Sri Lankanese, Australians,

Singaporeans, Iranians, Lebanese, Turks, Saudis, and French. In our communication sessions, people from all cultures insist that proper language separates the wealthy from the poor, the educated from the uneducated, the movers and shakers from the down-and-outers.

This book will help you prevent negative perceptions and reactions. You'll

- ▶ Improve the clarity of what you say or write.
- ▶ Learn tips or techniques to remember proper usage.
- ▶ Become aware of your own grammatical mistakes that annoy others and limit your social life.
- ▶ Correct mistakes when you write or speak so that you can get a better job—or hold on to the one you have.
- ▶ Remove obstacles to career advancement and make yourself more promotable.

You can correct deficiencies in a matter of a few hours or days of diligent study.

Confession: I'm lousy at interior design. And though I'd love to learn the skill, I fear that reading one good book on the subject wouldn't tell me all I need to know about it.

Grammar, on the other hand, *can* be learned from a book. I've designed this book so that you can quickly skim the chapter titles to find phrases that sound familiar to you—*and shouldn't!* That is, when you see a grammar error you always make, stop. Reflect on why it's wrong, and then review the examples in that section.

The Memory Tip at the end of each section provides a tip, rhyme, example, or rule of thumb to help you correct the mistake immediately. Some techniques are deliberately outlandish. That's because memory experts tell us that the more elaborate a visualization, for example, of someone's name with the face, the easier it will be to remember the name. That's the idea here—the more unusual the visualization or technique, the more likely it is that you'll remember it. And finally, some memory tips are simple, straightforward, cut-to-the-bone rules.

Booher's Rules of Business Grammar is not designed as a comprehensive "all you need to know" grammar text. (My earlier book *Good Grief, Good Grammar* provides that foundational information, and *E-Writing: 21st Century Tools for Effective Communication* outlines strategic steps in writing clear documents.) Rather, this quick book focuses on common errors so that you can read it today and speak or write correctly tomorrow.

Your job, your paycheck, your date, your mate—they may all depend on how well and how fast you rid yourself of the grammar gremlins holding you back. In fact, before you get started on Chapter 1 here, you may want to go to www.BoohersRules.com to assess your mastery of the subject. Then when you finish reading the book and return to the site to retake the assessment, you'll have a real sense of accomplishment. (In fact, drop us a note at mailroom@booher.com to let us know how much you improved your score after reading the book.)

For those of you who are already grammar gurus, you may polish a few of "the finer points" you've forgotten through the years. With these nuances of meanings within your command, you'll have a full range of expression at the tip of your tongue or touch of the keyboard. Let's get started.

BOOHER'S RULES

OF

BUSINESS GRAMMAR

PART 1

Verbosity About Verbs: The Big Blunders

When it comes to sports, you know what they say: no guts, no glory. When it comes to writing, a sentence without a verb is no sentence at all. Really. That's why the "really" I just wrote is no sentence. A sentence, by definition, must have a subject (what you're talking about) and a verb (what a subject *does*, *has*, or *is*). Verbs carry the action of the sentence.

For the most part, people put regular verbs in sentences without a problem. It's the irregular verbs that create the headaches. So we'll tackle the troublesome ones here.

1

Let's Dialogue About Verbing Words

TURNING PERFECTLY FINE NOUNS INTO VERBS

In case you haven't noticed, a number of new words are *trending* into the vocabulary, many of them verbs. They are *impacting* the way we handle our clients, *text-message* our buddies, and even *incent* our employees.

Managers become particularly adept at *globalizing* new trends and *fast-tracking* their way around obstacles like generally accepted grammar usage to gain competitive advantage. In fact, these managers often *incentivize* outstanding performers by complimenting them on their reports and proposals containing such usages. They often *dialogue* about important projects and hope the entire team *nets* the essentials.

Then, whether *downsized* or *right-sized*, teams can *strategize* organizational initiatives, *prioritize* divisional goals, *operationalize* tactical plans, *utilize* their best resources, *marginalize* any deficiencies in their systems, *institutionalize* project outcomes, *optimize* their opportunities, *mobilize* human talent, and *capitalize* on their investments.

Enough said.

Before you add an *–ing* or an *–ize* to a noun or coin a completely new word, consider checking the dictionary to see if a perfectly precise one already exists for the concept you want to convey.

MEMORY TIP

Save your memory! Use the strong, precise verbs that already exist.

2

"She Went Missing"

SUCKING THE LIFE OUT OF STRONG VERBS

The other extreme from creating new verbs on a whim involves smothering strong verbs with weaker ones.

Almost every day, TV broadcasters make announcements like this: "Sidney Lancaster went missing yesterday after leaving work at 6:00 in his red Toyota." Went missing? Is this like gone fishing or gone to the movies? Whatever happened to "Sidney is missing"? We don't know that he *went* anywhere. In fact, he may have been dragged kicking and screaming by an ax murderer.

How many times a week do reporters tell you to "take a listen"? Is this like walking into a department store and taking a number?

Okay, okay, I'll lay off reporters and broadcasters. These phrases from the e-mails of your colleagues may sound familiar as well. The following are not errors; they just weaken your writing.

Call and make a reservation. (Call and reserve?)
Run a test to see if . . . (Test to see if?)
Carry out experiments to . . . (Experiment?)
Perform an analysis of . . . (Analyze?)
Provide for the elimination of . . . (Eliminate?)
They experienced a reduction in . . . (They reduced?)

Make a visual examination of . . . (Investigate? Examine? See? Inspect?)

Strong verbs deserve a life of their own. Why sap their strength by turning them into nouns?

MEMORY TIP

The next time you hear, "She went missing," think voluntarily? AWOL? Hear that phrase as a reminder for strong verbs of your own.

3

Staying Regular

IRREGULAR VERBS

Since I travel frequently, I often have to drive a rental car in a strange city. When I grab a map and notice that the city forefathers had the good sense to lay out the streets in a pattern, I'm always grateful. For example, Washington, D.C., is easy to navigate. The numbered streets run north and south, and the lettered/named avenues flow east and west. It's a logical, if not exactly creative, pattern.

Whether we're pushing a cart down the grocery aisle, reviewing a Web site, or hanging wallpaper, patterns feel comfortable.

For the most part, verb patterns strike us the same way. We get used to them, and the vast majority of them roll off the tongue with ease:

I run. You run. Bill runs. We run. They run.

I talk. You talk. Bill talks. We talk. They talk.

I write checks. You write checks. She writes checks. We write checks. They write checks.

If you're talking in the past tense, the pattern is to add an *–ed* to the verb. For example: *hire, hired; cover, covered; interview, interviewed; chew, chewed; jump, jumped; approve, approved.*

I wrecked my car. You wrecked your car. Kilpatrick wrecked his car. We wrecked our car. They wrecked their car.

I identified the house. You identified the house. Kilpatrick identified the house. We identified the house. They identified the house.

I called the number. You called the number. Ziggy called the number. We called the number. They called the number.

But some verbs cause problems because they break the pattern—just like the city streets that branch off at a angle, change names three times without ever making a turn, or come to a dead end without warning.

Have you ever heard a four-year-old trying to follow the verb pattern with new vocabulary: "I buyed candy with my dollar" or "I runned home because that big dog was chasing me." They're following the pattern of adding an –ed, but those verbs don't follow the pattern. Instead, they're an exception to the rule.

Some common irregular verbs are listed in the chart below. The last four verbs in the chart are the most common irregular verbs, and some very smart people have difficulty remembering them: *do, go, come,* and *see.* (Yes, I agree—they're odd, weird, illogical, out of sync, fouled up. Scream at the washing machine or kick a punching bag. Just don't blame me.)

Present	Past	Past Participle
write	wrote	written
begin	began	begun
do	did	done

Present	Past	Past Participle
am	was	been
break	broke	broken
choose	chose	chosen
teach	taught	taught
drive	drove	driven
draw	drew	drawn
fly	flew	flown
grow	grew	grown
speak	spoke	spoken
do	did	done
go	went	gone
come	came	come
see	saw	seen

MEMORY TIP

You'll need to memorize these irregular verbs through use. For *do*, *go*, *come*, and *see*, refer to the next four chapters for specific memory aids.

4

"He Don't Understand"

THE IRREGULAR VERB *TO DO*

The most common error with the irregular verb *to do* occurs when making the first-person singular a contraction with *not*.

Incorrect:
> Pudge don't know what to do with his money.
> Spike don't remember his hometown very well.
> Gertrude don't travel internationally.

Correct:
> Pudge doesn't know what to do with his money.
> Spike doesn't remember his hometown very well.
> Gertrude doesn't travel internationally.

Here's how the verb looks in the present tense:

Present Tense (*to do*):

I don't know what to do.	We don't know what to do.
You don't know what to do. (singular)	You don't know what to do. (plural)
Pudge *doesn't* know what to do.	They don't know what to do.

No one mistakenly says, "He do." If a friend asks who has change for a $100 bill, you might answer: "I do," or "You do," or "We do," or "They do," or "He does." No one ever responds, "He do." To answer the same question in the negative, simply add a *not* to the root word *does*. "He doesn't." "She doesn't." "Spike doesn't."

▼

MEMORY TIP

Think wedding vows: "I do." "You do." "He does." Then make each word negative: "I don't." "You don't." "He doesn't" or "she doesn't."

5

"They Had Went to My Office Earlier in the Day"

THE IRREGULAR VERB TO GO

The irregular verb *to go* gives people problems most often in the present and past tenses. That is, they mistakenly use *went* with the helping verbs *have*, *has*, and *had*.

Incorrect:
> Fritz had went to the Paris exhibit last year.
>
> They had went to that conference earlier in the year.
>
> I have went to the major power brokers to try to negotiate the deal.

Correct:
> Fritz had gone to the Paris exhibit last year.
>
> They had gone to that conference earlier in the year.
>
> I have gone to the major power brokers to try to negotiate the deal.

Here's how the verb looks in the past tense:

Present Perfect Tense (*to go*)
(started in the past and continuing in the present):

I have gone to my manager about the problem and am waiting for a decision.

You (singular—an individual) have gone to your manager about the problem, so be patient.

Fritz has gone to the manager about the problem and is waiting for a decision.

We have gone to the manager about the problem and are waiting for a decision.

You (plural—a group) have gone to the manager about the problem, so be patient.

They have gone to the manager about the problem so they should be patient.

Past Perfect Tense (*to go*)
(started in the past and ended before a specific time in the past):

I had gone to Boston for the conference, but I missed the party on Friday.

You (singularly—an individual) had gone to the conference, but evidently you missed the party on Friday.

Hannah had gone to the conference, but evidently she missed the party on Friday.

We had gone to the conference, but we missed the party on Friday.

You (plural—a group) had gone to the conference, but evidently you missed the party on Friday.

They had gone to the conference, but they missed the party on Friday.

MEMORY TIP

Remember that the classic movie is titled *Gone with the Wind*, not *Went with the Wind*.

6

"He Come Back From Overseas Early"

THE IRREGULAR VERB TO COME

The most common error with the irregular verb *to come* occurs in the past tense.

Incorrect:

Eldora come home from work early yesterday.

The members come up with a new approach to the problem last month.

We come to the airport to meet the client, but she had already taken a cab.

Correct:

Eldora came home from work early yesterday.

The members came up with a new approach to the problem last month.

We came to the airport to meet the client, but she had already taken a cab.

The irregular verb *to come* has this strange pattern:

Present Tense:

They come home late from work every day.

Past Tense:

They came home late from work last week.

Present Perfect Tense:

They have come home late from work every day this month.

Past Perfect Tense:

They had come home late from work every day last year, so that's why they began to look for a house near downtown.

MEMORY TIP

Past has an *a* in it. *Came* has an *a* in it. Use *came* only when you're talking about the past. *Come* has an *o* in it. *Come* represents the present, now, with an *o* in it.

$$C A M E = P A S T \qquad C O M E = N O W$$

Example:

Trixy came (past) by for lunch.

Trixy comes (now) by every day for lunch.

7

"I Seen Him Leave"

THE IRREGULAR VERB TO SEE

Another irregular verb that wreaks havoc is *to see*. The typical problem occurs in the past tense, with *seen* (and the failure to use the helping verb *have* or *has* to accompany *seen*).

Incorrect:
> We seen them go into the building.
> Winnifred, Horatio, and Ebeneezer seen the sales team earlier this
> morning.
> They seen our repair trucks in the area.
> I seen the manager talking to the team in his office.

Correct (if talking about an event in the past):
> We saw them go into the building today.
> Winnifred, Horatio, and Ebeneezer saw the sales team earlier this
> week.
> They saw our repair trucks in the area.
> I saw the manager talking to the team in his office.

Correct (if talking about something that has happened in the past and is continuing or routinely happens):

> We have seen them go into the building on previous occasions.
>
> Winnifred, Horatio, and Ebeneezer have seen the sales team earlier this week.
>
> They have seen our repair trucks in the area.
>
> I have seen the manager talking to the team in his office frequently.

MEMORY TIP

Seen sounds like *scene*—from a movie. Just as you need a ticket for a movie *scene*, you need a *have* for a sentence *seen*.

8

Lie or Lay Before I Knock You Off Your Feet

THE *LIE/LAY* LIMBO

The most common error with these two verbs pops up in sentences like these:

Incorrect:

Wilmo is going to lay down for a few minutes to rest.

That paperwork has been laying on my desk for days.

Her photo laid on my kitchen table for weeks before I could bear to put it away.

In these instances, somebody or something is reclining. The verb meaning to recline is *to lie*. (*To lie* also means to tell a falsehood, but nobody makes an error with that use.)

Correct:

Wilmo is going to lie down for a few minutes to rest.

That paperwork has been lying on my desk for days.

Her photo lay on my kitchen table for weeks before I could bear to put it away.

To lay means to place something. Once you place something, it then lies or reclines: "I laid the photo on my desk yesterday; it has been lying there ever since."

These two verbs make you wish for a site map for tracking purposes so that you don't lose your way through the discussion. In fact, we're so used to navigating the Internet that the site-map analogy may be the best method to understand these overlapping words in their very different meanings and time frames.

Notice where these maps intersect; that is, notice where the words look alike but have an entirely different meaning.

Site Map for *Lie*

Noun: a falsehood			
		lie	Brunhilda told a lie.
Verb: to tell a falsehood			
	Present	lie	We often lie if we are embarrassed.
	Past	lied	Mortimer lied yesterday.
	Present participle	lied	Mortimer has lied on numerous occasions.
	Past participle	lied	Mortimer had lied on numerous occasions before he was arrested yesterday.
Verb: to recline			
	Present	lie	We lie down for a nap every day.
			Fritz's home lies in the foothills of the state.
	Past	lay	We lay down for a nap at noon yesterday.

			The unsigned check lay on his desk for a week.
Present participle	lying		Eldora is lying down for a nap every day after her chemo treatments.
			The carpet has been lying untouched for a month since its installation.
Past participle	lain		Fritz had lain down for a nap and was unavailable to see us when we visited.
			The contract had lain on his desk for weeks before he finally signed it.

Site Map for *Lay*

Verb: to place			
Present	lay		They lay walkways around each building they construct.
Past	laid		They laid walkways around the building across the street.
Present participle	laid		They have laid walkways around the building this week.
Past participle	laid		They had laid walkways around the building before Trixy ordered them to dig tunnels and canals.

To sum up, you *lay* (place) items down. Once placed, items or people *lie* (recline).

MEMORY TIP

Lie is about the BIG *I*. To keep from getting lost on the map, distinguish between these two verbs right up front. *Lie* has *I* in the center—and that's usually the case about *to lie* in all its forms. It's typically about people. People lie (tell a falsehood) to save their ego, their job, or a relationship. They also lie (recline) to protect themselves—to save their strength or energy. Once you understand the meaning of the BIG I, your sentence can refer to any person (or also an object) that's doing the lying or reclining.

Placing, on the other hand, has an *a* in it. Likewise, *lay* has an *a*. After you choose the correct word for its meaning in the present tense, put the verb through its paces to get the right tense for the intended time frame.

9

He Came, He Saw, He Conquered

DON'T BE LAX ABOUT TENSE CHANGES

Evidently Julius Caesar, the Roman general and statesman, knew what he was doing when he arrived on the scene: he came, he saw, he conquered. When the rest of us change verb tenses without cause, it raises questions—either about our confidence or about our grammar.

Verbs have tenses to reflect the time: present, past, future. "Pongo is not feeling well this morning" (present). "So he may go home from work this afternoon following his client teleconference" (future). "Yesterday, he left early to play golf" (past). "And I understand that he is planning to travel to a convention on Friday" (present). "Therefore, he will miss three consecutive staff meetings" (future). These clearly appropriate tense changes reflect different times.

The following sentence is a careless tense change without reason:

Incorrect:

Her e-mail included pricing; it also provides a volume-discount schedule.

Correct:

> Her e-mail includes pricing; it also provides a volume-discount schedule.

Clarity becomes an issue in the following passage:

> Ebeneezer's expense report *shows* charges of $487 for the June trip. Dilbert's expense report *lists* charges of $439 for the trip. Eldora's report *indicates* expenses of $502 for the training program. Percival's expense report *showed* charges of $898 for the training.

Question: did Percival travel at the same time the other three people did? Is the writer pointing out a discrepancy between the lower travel expenses submitted by his traveling companions Ebeneezer, Dilbert, and Eldora? Or, did Percival travel earlier than the other people? Is Percival padding his expense account?

But hold on a minute before you jump to conclusions: Did you notice that *showed* is in the past tense? If Percival traveled at an earlier date, maybe the airfare or the hotel cost more at that time. Maybe the point of the information about the expenses is that recent travel costs have been reduced.

My point: unnecessary tense changes create questions. Here's another confusing passage.

Incorrect:

> Phone inquiries were entered into the system as they come in and appear on the screen in front of the agents taking the calls. Agents have been trained to solicit only contact information. Customer service agents should transfer callers within 30 seconds. A third-party Web site will take the actual orders.

When in this process do phone inquiries get entered into the system? Are these entries part of the current process or an explanation of earlier steps? Because the tenses vary throughout, it sounds as though the phone entries happen prior to the present step in the process. Is the point here to outline steps to follow to get a job done—or to explain past action?

Correct:

> Phone inquiries *enter* the system as they come in and *appear* on the screen in front of the agents taking the calls. Customer service agents *solicit* only contact information. Agents *transfer* callers within 30 seconds. A third-party Web site *takes* the actual orders.

In this rewritten passage, all the tenses match—present tense. All the action is clearly part of a current procedure.

If you *intend* to change tenses in the middle of a sentence or a passage, fine. No problem. Don't let me stand in your way. By all means, you know what point you intend to make. Just don't change tenses randomly. Such a change can cause misreading about what happens when.

To save time—yours and your reader's—tenses should accurately reflect time.

▼

MEMORY TIP

Time is money. Be as careful with your tenses as with your tens.

10

"If I Was You . . ."

WISHFUL THINKING AND
THE SUBJUNCTIVE MOOD

Nine times out of ten, when someone starts off with, "If I was you," they're about to give you advice. And not only are you about to hear advice—maybe bad advice—but you're hearing bad grammar. Being the courteous, rational person you probably are, I'm sure you listen despite the mood.

No, I'm not talking about whether you feel surly or sad. I'm talking about sentence moods: indicative, imperative, and subjunctive.

Indicative-Mood Verbs, the Most Common,
Are Used to State Facts or Opinions or to Ask Questions:
Brunhilda chimes in too late on teleconferences.
Did Mortimer twiddle his thumbs rather than market the Webinar?

Imperative-Mood Verbs Give Commands:
Redesign our ad campaign before the Super Bowl.
Stop this nonsense and approve my million-dollar raise.
Close the door.

Subjunctive-Mood Sentences State Conditions That Are Contrary to Fact or Highly Unlikely (they also express strong wishes, demands, or commands, but more about that in the next chapter):

> If she were a billionaire, she would fund cancer research. (She's not a billionaire.)
>
> If I were CEO of that company, I'd hire 200 more salespeople next month. (I'm not the CEO.)

Incorrect:

> If I was you, I would resign.

Correct:

> If I were you, I would resign. (I'm not you.)

Incorrect:

> Pongo walked into the gym as if he was a Greek god.

Correct:

> Pongo walked into the gym as if he were a Greek god. (He's not a Greek god.)

In typical situations when the "if" part may actually be true, the verb following I or he/she remains *was*.

> If Fritz was told about the trouble in Atlanta, I guess he forgot it. (He may have been told.)
>
> If the caller was a client, Gertrude must have not recognized the name. (The caller may have been a client, but Gertrude still didn't recognize the name.)

MEMORY TIP

When you hear phrases like, "If I were you, what I'd do is . . . ," you know you're about to get advice. What are you tempted to do with bad advice? Reverse it. Do the same with subjunctive-mood verbs in phrases such as "If I were you. . . ."

11

Pushy People Demanding Their Way

THE SUBJUNCTIVE MOOD CONTINUED

Are you still with me? Good. Subjunctive-mood verbs also express strong wishes, demands, concessions, and resolutions. These verbs follow in the minor clause after such words as *command*, *demand*, *insist*, *order*, *recommend*, *require*, *wish*, and *suggest*.

Incorrect:

I wish she was able to transfer to headquarters.

Correct:

I wish she were able to transfer to headquarters.

Incorrect:

Mortimer tiptoed through the trade show as though networking was a nasty business.

Correct:

Mortimer tiptoed through the trade show as though networking were a nasty business. (Networking brings in viable leads.)

Other Examples:

The manager demanded that he leave the building.

Ziggy recommended that Daffy give the presentation.

Orilla moved that the meeting adjourn.

Snuffy insists that the manager write the apology.

The present-tense subjunctive is formed by dropping the *–s* from the third-person singular. (Example: "Gertrude manages" becomes "Gertrude manage.")

The past-tense subjunctive is indistinguishable from the past-tense indicative used to state facts or ask questions. No problem there.

The one big irregularity to all the above: the verb *to be.*

Subjunctive-mood present tense of *to be*: *be* (just the one odd word)

Subjunctive-mood past tense of *to be*: *were*

Normally, you say, "Fritz *was*" or "They *were*." But when you are ranting, raving, or resolving, you switch to *be*.

Examples:

I insist that Fritz *be* promoted.

Dilbert required that Ebeneezer *be* present for the meeting.

Eldora has demanded that her boss *be* fired for incompetence.

The report suggested that the team *be* exiled in cyberspace.

Managers suggest that new hires *be* trained by noon on the first day.

We are resolved that Mortimer *be* comfortable with the new regulations.

I urged that the price *be* discounted at least 20 percent.

Executives demand that engineers *be* good presenters.

In essence, these *be* constructions sound similar to command forms (imperative mood) of the verb: "Be careful." "Be quiet." "Be thorough." "Be specific." "Be brief." "Be seated." If this switching to the word *be* sounds odd to you, consider the word *should* inserted in front of it: "Executives demand that engineers (should) be good presenters."

Dilbert demanded that Fritz write the reports. (*should write*)
Ebeneezer urged that the team negotiate the cruise fares. (*should negotiate*)
Eldora insisted that Mortimer fire his brother-in-law. (*should fire*)
We are resolved that the teams collect all funds by June 30. (*should collect*)

Incorrect:

The client requirement is that all consultants are financially literate.

Correct:

The client requirement is that all consultants be financially literate.

Incorrect:

He demands that the report is mailed rather than sent electronically.

Correct:

He demands that the report be mailed rather than sent electronically.

Note: The subjunctive mood is found only in the minor (subordinate) clause, never in the main clause, of the sentence.

MEMORY TIP

Subjunctive sounds like *subjective*. Let the subjunctive mood remind you of subjective emotions: demands, urges, and wishes. Just as emotions frequently reverse people's actions, the subjunctive mood reverses the normal verb.

12

"There's Problems With That!"

EXPLETIVE DELETED

Rest easy. I'm not about to launch into obscene language here. An expletive is a word that has nothing grammatically to do with the rest of the sentence. You've heard of *Phantom of the Opera*, no doubt. Consider this issue *Phantom of the Sentence*: sentences with a fake subject sitting in the typical subject slot.

The most frequent expletives are sentence beginnings such as *there is*, *there was*, *there were*, *there are*, *it is*, or *it was*. Think of these beginning words (*there*, *it*) as fillers without meaning. "There were six people riding in our car." The *there* is meaningless, a phantom subject. The real subject of the sentence is *six people*. (*Six people* were riding in our car.)

Another example: "It is a problem to suggest tax revolt." *It* is a phantom subject, meaningless. *It* stands for the entire concept: "To suggest tax revolt is a problem."

There's no problem in using expletives—as I just did in this sentence—as long as you understand that those words aren't the true subject of your sentence and select the right verbs to go with the real subject.

Incorrect:

There's problems with retaining law firms over the Internet. (*Problems* is the subject of this sentence, so the sentence needs a plural verb.)

Correct:

There are problems with retaining law firms over the Internet.

Better:

Retaining law firms over the Internet presents problems.

Beginning a sentence with an expletive *there* or *it* gives the impression of timidly backing into the key idea. It's better to express most thoughts with a stronger opening.

Weak:

There were whirling gizmos that attracted attention from every buyer.

Stronger:

Whirling gizmos attracted attention from every buyer.

Weak:

There were some who negotiated fares better than 70 percent off retail price.

Stronger:

Some negotiated fares better than 70 percent off retail price.

Weak:

It is a big disappointment to lose the game.

Stronger:

Losing the game is a big disappointment.

MEMORY TIP

Consider a mother's "there, there" to a crying baby. The words are comforting but meaningless. The same is true with expletives—they're meaningless. Find the real subject, and select the verb accordingly.

13

"I Wish I May, I Wish I Might . . . Could You Tell Me Which Verb to Use Tonight?"

THE MAY/MIGHT DILEMMA

Dusty Springfield, a pop star of the 1960s, may still be "just wishin', and hopin'," but the rest of us need to know the right words to use when things are distinct possibilities at home and work.

May means that things are possible, even likely. *Might* means that there's less likelihood of something happening.

> I may get to take an African safari. (possible on my next trip to Africa)
> I might get to take an African safari. (not very likely, but I'm wishing and hoping)
> Percival may have to resign if he can't explain the errors. (possible, even likely)
> Percival might have to resign if he can't explain the errors. (unlikely, teasing him)

Now let's add one more layer of complexity: *Might* is also the past tense of *may*. In those situations, the degree of possibility is not the criterion for using *might*. If the other verbs in the sentence are past tense, *may* becomes *might* (past tense).

> The report *stated* that the buyers *might* conduct plant tours unannounced. (We don't know how probable the tours are.)
>
> Wall Street analysts *indicated* that investors *might* be squeamish about our stock. (Who knows how likely they'll be to react negatively?)
>
> Percival *said* he *might* resign. (Darned if we know if he will or won't.)

So what's a person to do with a *may* or *might* choice? Like Dusty Springfield in her classic song, decide if you're just wishing and hoping or if you have a real shot at your dream.

▼

MEMORY TIP

Link this *may-might* dilemma to Dusty Springfield's hit, and you'll be humming the criterion for choosing the correct word: What's the likelihood? *May* implies that things are more likely than *might* does.

14

"Sue Is One Who . . ."

THE ONE OF A KIND OR
ONE OF A CATEGORY ARGUMENT

Select the wrong verb in these sentences and you've changed the meaning dramatically. Should you say, "Trixy is one of the managers who falsifies time sheets" or "Trixy is one of the managers who falsify time sheets"?

The dilemma is deciding which verb goes with the subject *who*. *Who* is an indefinite pronoun, meaning that it can refer to either *managers* or *Trixy*. Flip the sentence around to reword it but retain the original meaning. Then the verb choice will become clear:

> Of the managers, Trixy is the one falsifying time sheets. (If this is the meaning and you are writing "Trixy is one of the managers who falsifies time sheets," you are correct. *Who* refers to *one*.)
>
> Of the managers falsifying time sheets, Trixy is one. (If this is the meaning and you are writing, "Trixy is one of the managers who falsify time sheets," you are correct. *Who* refers to *managers*.)

Let's try another example: "Wilmo lost one of his accounts that (generates or generate?) hundreds of leads annually." Which verb should it be? Reword the sentence to verify your meaning, and the correct verb will surface:

Of his *accounts that generate* hundreds of leads annually, Wilmo lost one. (Is this the intended meaning? If so, *that* refers to *accounts* and needs a plural verb: *generate*. It's not likely that this is the meaning here.)

Of his accounts, Wilmo lost *one that generates* hundreds of leads annually. (Is this the intended meaning? If so, *that* refers to one and needs a singular verb: *generates*.)

▼

MEMORY TIP

To find the right verb, flip the sentence, keeping the meaning intact. The correct verb will rise to the occasion.

15

Separation Anxiety

SUBJECTS AND VERBS THAT GET SPLIT APART

Consider the sentence a long shoelace, with the subject on one end and the verb on the other. No matter how many eyelets you snake that shoelace through across your foot, at some point those two ends of the shoelace (the subject and verb) must meet and tie together.

Most often, subjects come at the beginning of a sentence, followed closely by the verb. "Dilbert danced." "The manager signed the check." But sometimes talkers and writers begin with the subject and then get sidetracked, tossing in other descriptive words and phrases before they finish their main point about the subject.

These extra words that separate the subject and the verb confuse things. People choose the wrong verb form to match a word that's not the real subject.

Incorrect:

The secret to hiring the best people as marketing and sales team members for small mom-and-pop organizations are finding people who have once been in business for themselves. (*Members* and *organizations* are not the subjects; they're objects of prepositions.)

Correct:

> The *secret* to hiring the best people as marketing and sales team members for small mom-and-pop organizations *is* finding people who have once been in business for themselves.

Occasionally, you may even flout tradition and flip your sentence so that the subject comes at the end of the sentence. Again, who am I to stand in your way? Writer's choice. But if you flip, flop the correct verb in place:

Incorrect:

> After our analysis of the results of the customer satisfaction survey was several suggestions submitted by the board of directors. (*Analysis*, *results*, and *survey* are not subjects. They're objects of prepositions.)

Correct:

> After our analysis of the results of the customer satisfaction survey *were* several *suggestions* submitted by the board of directors.

You can catch this error quickly by cutting the flesh off the bone, leaving just the sentence skeleton: subject and verb. Make the subject and verb match, either singular or plural.

MEMORY TIP

No matter where they fall, find the two ends of the shoelace (subject and verb) and tie them together.

16

Which End Is Up?

COMPLEMENTS OF THE VERB OR THE CHEF

Which of the following sentences is correct?

A good source of beta-carotene is carrots.
Carrots are a good source of beta-carotene.

Linking verbs are those that are not complete within themselves. They simply serve as a bridge, linking the subject to the idea on the other side. Sentences with linking verbs (*is*, *are*, *was*, *were*, *become*, *appears*, *seems*, *sounds*, *smells*) sometimes have a plural subject and a singular verb or vice versa. In those cases, always make the verb agree with the subject, not the complement.

So both sentences above are correct: "A good source is . . ." and "Carrots are . . ."

Another example:

Correct:

Hunting and golfing appear to be his retirement goal. (plural)

Correct:

His retirement goal appears to be hunting and golfing. (singular)

The common mistake with such sentences is making a U-turn before choosing the verb. That is, people think faster than they speak.

So they speed to the end of the sentence, hear the plural complement, back up mentally, and insert a plural verb. Illegal turn.

If the sentence sounds strange with a plural on one end as subject and a singular on the other as complement, recast it so that the two ends "balance" as either plurals or singulars.

Other examples:

Laptops are our hottest products for the season.
Our hottest product for the season is the laptop.
Jamale Jackson and Beulah Brownwood appear to be the winning team.
The winning team appears to be Jamale Jackson and Beulah Brownwood.

MEMORY TIP

Visualize these sentences as those one-way entrance gates at rental car lots, where the sign reads: "Do not back up. Backing up will cause severe injury to tires." Start at one end of an idea and drive to the other end, making the subject and verb match as you go. If you drive to the end and find a plural noun, and then try to back up and change the verb to a plural, you'll cause serious injury to your sentence.

17

Acting Alone or With Accomplices?

VERBS AFTER COLLECTIVE NOUNS

Collective nouns name people, things, or ideas as a group: *committee, management, team, audience, equipment, organization*. In most situations, collective nouns act as a single unit, so they need a singular verb.

Incorrect:

> The jury have decided to give her probation rather than jail time.
> Our club are donating its facilities as a homeless shelter during the emergency.

Correct:

> Management is disappointed in the sales volume for the year.
> Our team has met its deadline each quarter.
> The equipment needs servicing daily.

On occasion, however, these collective nouns can refer to the members of a group individually. When that's the case, make the verb plural.

The team argued among itself about how to present the results.
The committee have spoken against one another to various reporters.

However, sentences like the last two generally sound better if reworded:

The team *members* argued among themselves about how to present the results.
The committee *members* have spoken against one another to various reporters.

MEMORY TIP

A collection agency becomes one big bulldog going after all unpaid debts. Likewise, a collective noun acts as one single agent requiring one singular verb.

18

None of Your Business

DEFINITELY INDEFINITE PRONOUNS

You can be undecided about donuts, a Saturday night date, or client data. But verbs after indefinite pronouns call for a decision. Indefinite pronouns are those such as *none*, *most*, *all*, *one*, *some*, *more*, or *any*. Verbs after these pronouns can be singular or plural, depending on what noun or pronoun they replace or refer to in context.

Most of my equipment *is* under warranty.
Most of my computers *are* under warranty.
Some of my money *is* invested in mutual funds.
Some of my retirement funds *are* invested in annuities.
Some of the bombs *have been set* to detonate at noon.
Some of the paint *has been leaking*.
All of the paperwork *is* complete.
All of the contracts *are* complete.
None of the building *has been damaged*.
None of the employees *have been complaining*.

If you're going to get any grief about this, somebody somewhere will probably want to lecture you about *none*, insisting that *none* means "not one." Mrs. McCullough, seventh-grade English, bless her heart, pursed her lips and insisted on that until the day she died—or at least until I graduated. But *none* can mean "not one" or "not any." More frequently than not, people use it to mean "not any."

> None of the cars are damaged. (not any)
> None of the cars is damaged. (not even one—how remarkable)
> None of the coins are missing. (not any)
> None of the coins is missing. (not even one—amazing)

MEMORY TIP

With indefinite pronouns, be definite. Consider the context to determine the meaning, and then make the verb choice either singular or plural.

▼

19

Total 'Em Up

VERBS WITH TIME, MONEY, QUANTITIES,
FRACTIONS, AND PERCENTAGES

The common mistake with expressions such as *20 dollars* or *40 hours* is to think of them slipping through your hand or ticking by one by one. While they do disappear fast, in most situations, consider these expressions to be one total amount.

When thought of as a single unit, expressions of time, money, and quantity take a singular verb.

> Twenty gallons is all my gas tank holds.
>
> Forty hours is now considered a short workweek for the typical company.
>
> Twenty-two percent represents a small portion of the voting population.
>
> Six acres was all that he inherited from his parents.

MEMORY TIP

In math, you first learn to add numbers. In English, you do the same thing: One composite number (a total number of hours, dollars, miles, or whatever) expressed as a single total gets a singular verb.

20

The Kaleidoscope Effect

A AND *THE* BEFORE AMOUNTS

As a kid, did you ever look through a kaleidoscope to see all the different colors, shapes, and designs blend into one another as you turned the lens from side to side? By turning the lens in one direction, you could make the shapes expand. By turning the lens in the opposite direction, you could make the shapes melt back on top of each other into one larger design.

Placing the article *a* or *the* in front of a noun that means a fraction or an amount has that same kaleidoscope effect. Those articles either expand or contract the meaning of the amounts that follow.

Let's say your boss calls you into his or her office and says, "I want to talk to you about *a number* of things?" Would you bet on a one-item agenda or several? Several, right? Likewise, the article *a* before one of these "amount" words typically expands the meaning—makes the meaning plural. *The* narrows the meaning to a single total: "*The number* of people attending the conference is small."

In a nutshell, the verb choice depends on whether the nouns in the group act as a group or individually. The article in front of them (*a* or *the*) tells the story by expanding or contracting the meaning.

A number of people *have called* to complain. (many acting individually—plural)

But: The number who asked to have their service disconnected *is*
small. (one total referred to as a group—singular)

MEMORY TIP

Visualize the kaleidoscope effect of *a* number or *the* number as it
expands or limits the meaning of your subject.

21

The Seesaw Effect

EITHER/OR, NEITHER/NOR,
NOT ONLY/BUT ALSO

Consider both halves of *either/or*, *neither/nor*, and *not only/but also* subjects as if they are separate elements.

▶ Subjects linked by *either/or* and *neither/nor* usually take a singular verb.

▶ If one subject is plural and the other subject is singular, make the verb agree with the closest subject.

Unless there is a reason not to do so, it's better to write the plural subject second, because the construction will not grate on your ear.

Either your manager or your mentor *has* made a mistake in recommending this job assignment.

Either the salespeople in Atlanta or the salespeople in Los Angles *have* misunderstood the contest rules.

Neither friends nor relatives *understand* the loneliness of divorce like someone who has experienced it.

Neither a friend nor a relative *understands* the loneliness of divorce like someone who has experienced it.

Not only Horatio but also my team members *are* looking forward to the presentation. (the typical and preferred way to structure this situation, with the plural subject closest to the verb)

Not only my team members but also Horatio *is* looking forward to the presentation. (atypical structure, obviously meant to emphasize Horatio's state of mind more than that of the team members)

MEMORY TIP

Think of this construction as a playground seesaw. The individual items on each end balance but are separate.

The *either/or, neither/nor,* and *not only/but also* constructions mimic the seesaw. The words on both sides of the link are separate subjects that "balance." If one subject weighs more (is plural), the verb must match it to stay in balance.

PART 2

Pesky Pronouns: The Understudies

Pronouns never have starring roles in sentences; instead, they are stand-ins for nouns. You can say, "Eldora has hired all four of those new managers" or "*She* has hired all four of them." You can say, "Brunhilda's workstation always looks like a cyclone hit Brunhilda's workstation" or "*Her* workstation always looks like a cyclone hit it."

In the theater, of course, an understudy plays only one role—not three. That is, if *he* stands in for the Duke of Featherbone, *he* can't also play the role of the Princess Prianna. The same is true for pronouns. Because of their physical characteristics, they can play only a limited number of roles. They can stand in for the subject or an object of a sentence, but not both.

Therein lies the crux of the problem—matching the understudy to the appropriate role in the sentence.

22

"Just Between You and I"

THE CASE FOR OBJECTIVE PRONOUNS

As the owner of a communication training company, I've literally been reading other people's mail for 27 years. By far, the most frequently misused pronoun is the one in a sentence like this:

Incorrect:
Just between you and I, we all know who runs this place.

Let's continue the understudy analogy further: The understudy pronoun *I* is playing the wrong role here. Hearing a pronoun error like this is equivalent to watching a play and having a 70-year-old male run on stage to play the part of the teenage girl.

Here are the actors that can stand in for subjects: *I, you, he, she, it, we, they, who,* and *whoever.*

These are the actors that can stand in for objects (primarily objects of prepositions and direct and indirect objects): *me, you, him, her, it, us, them, whom,* and *whomever.*

You'll notice that *you* and *it* can play either role—subjects or objects. They make the big bucks. Also, we have a whole slew of indefinite pronouns that can play both roles: *anyone, everybody, none, some, all, many, one, them, these, those, this, that, what, any, each, both, nobody, few, others, several,* and *anyone.* For the most part, these don't cause problems. It's the actors that play only one role that create the headaches.

Back to "Just between you and I, we all know who runs this place": the *I* is standing in for an object of the preposition *between,* but the pronoun *I* can accept only "subject" roles. So the proper noun in this sentence is *me.* (For some reason, people seem to think that *I* sounds more sophisticated than *me.*)

Correct:

Just between you and me, we all know who runs this place.

Incorrect:

Please call Ebeneezer and I with the test results. (object of the verb—*me* has to be the stand-in here)

He mailed multiple invoices to Percival, three clients, and I. (object of the preposition—*me* has to be the stand-in here)

Leave the other people out of a sentence and let your ear do the work. The correct pronoun will become obvious. You would never say, "Please call I with the test results" or "He mailed multiple invoices to I."

Correct:

Please call me with the test results.

He mailed multiple invoices to me.

Memory Tip

Omit the other people in the sentence, and trust your ear to select the right objective pronoun.

23

"Me and Pongo Know Him"

THE CASE FOR NOMINATIVE PRONOUNS

Maybe this currently common error has to do with the Me Generation in the workplace. Or maybe the reason is that the Boomers have focused on *their* entrepreneurial ventures as they retire. Or maybe . . . well, enough philosophizing about why this usage pops up daily on the airwaves and streets during interviews with politicians, pundits, and power brokers of all sorts. Let's just jump on it and quash it before it grows.

When it comes to pronouns, remember what your momma always told you about being considerate and putting others first. Make your momma proud: Put others first, then follow with pronouns that can play the role of subjects. Technically, they're called nominative pronouns. (Refer to the entry on "Just Between You and I" for the acting analogy.)

Incorrect:

Me and Eldora have a lunch appointment Tuesday. (Would you ever say, "Me has a lunch appointment Tuesday?" Of course not, so *me* can't play the role of subject. Get *me* out of there!)

Her, Pongo, and Wilmo's sales staff introduced the product to prospects throughout the region. (Would you ever say, "Her introduced the product to prospects throughout the region?" Not on your life. Get *her* out of the subject role.)

Correct:

Eldora and I have a lunch appointment Tuesday.

Pongo, Wilmo's sales staff, and she introduced the product to prospects throughout the region.

MEMORY TIP

To get the correct subject pronoun, test the sentence by dropping the other names, and let your ear do the rest.

24

Me, Myself, and I

REFLEXIVE PRONOUNS FLEXING THEIR MUSCLES

Somebody somewhere sometime must have told a class of students that the "self" pronouns (reflexive pronouns), such as *myself*, *yourself*, and *ourselves*, sound more elegant or sophisticated than the plain garden variety. Then viral networking took over.

Everywhere you go, you hear incorrect comments such as these:

Incorrect:

Jordan and *myself* manage that department.

Heather, Tommy, and *myself* are involved in that meeting.

Why don't Frank, Sol, and *yourself* accompany Melinda to Atlanta?

Whatever happened to plain old *me*? A sentence must contain another noun or pronoun to which this *self* refers. If *I* is not already in the sentence, it's incorrect to add *myself*. If *Susan* is not already mentioned in the sentence, then it's incorrect to stuff *herself* in there.

Again, leave out the other people, and let your ear do the work. You would never say, "*Myself* is involved in that meeting." Neither would you say, "Why don't *yourself* accompany Melinda to Atlanta?"

Correct:

> Jordan and I manage that department.
>
> Heather, Tommy, and I are involved in that meeting.
>
> Why don't Frank, Sol, and you accompany Melinda to Atlanta?

A good reason, on the other hand, to toss in a *self* pronoun is to add emphasis. Consider it a raised voice: "I *myself* told him about the problem!" (meaning: How could he claim that he doesn't know about the problem? Certainly he knows because I personally told him!)

Get adamant. Flex your muscle the next time somebody emails you a misused highfaluting *–self* pronoun when they need only the simple *I*, or *me*, or *he*, or *she*.

MEMORY TIP

Have you ever heard the line, "I'm so busy that I'm meeting myself coming and going"? That's a correct usage: *myself* refers to the *I* that's already in the sentence.

25

To Whom It May Concern

WHO VERSUS WHOM

At the risk of being redundant here, let's go back to the acting analogy. *Who* and *whoever* play the role of subjects whenever they come on stage. *Whom* and *whomever* play the part of objects when they enter the theater. To solve most dilemmas, simplify, simplify, simplify. Identify the nearby verb, and then circle back to find the subject that goes with it. Strip down a sentence clause by clause.

> The manager asked whoever had the correct phone number to call. (*Whoever* plays the role of subject to the verb *had* in the minor clause.)
> You can make charitable contributions to whomever you wish. (*Whomever* plays the role of object of the preposition *to.*)

Granted, some sentences with *whom* sound stuffy, even though they're correct: "To whom did you wish to speak?" (You did wish to speak to whom. *Whom* plays the role of object—the object of the preposition *to.*) Rewording the sentence to end with the preposition sounds a little less stuffy: "Whom did you want to speak to?" Or, you can reword the sentence altogether: "Who are you calling, please?" It's incorrect, but far less stuffy for casual conversation.

As a side note, the use of the formal *whom* and *whomever* is fast disappearing from the language (probably because so few people use them correctly). That's one way to tackle a grammar problem—live long enough for the correct usage to become archaic.

▼

MEMORY TIP

Substitute *he* (the subject word) and *him* (the object wo) for *who* and *whom* and let your ear do the rest. If *he* sounds right, use *who* or *whoever*. If *him* sounds right, use *whom* or *whomever*.

Example: "Wilmo has notified the boss, (*whom* or *who?*) he likes, that the work is complete." (Reword: Wilmo has notified the boss that the work is complete. He likes him/whom.) Correct: "Wilmo has notified the boss, whom he likes, that the work is complete."

Example: "For (*who* or *whom?*) was this raise intended?" (Reword: This raise was intended for him/whom.) Correct: "For whom was this raise intended?"

26

"She's Taller Than Me"

PRONOUNS AFTER *THAN*

Want to burn off an extra pound while we're talking about height? Hang on a minute.

Which is correct?

We order supplies from Continental more often than them.
We order supplies from Continental more often than they.

Actually, both are correct. But the two sentences have different meanings. The first sentence means, "We order supplies from Continental more often than *we order from* them." The second sentence means, "We order supplies from Continental more often than they *order from Continental.*"

To make the correct pronoun choice after *than* or *as*, insert the omitted words and your ears will do the rest. Which of the next two sentences is correct?

Ziggy knows more about politics than me.
Ziggy knows more about politics than I.

Either: "Ziggy knows more about politics than I (know)." Or "Ziggy knows more about politics than (she knows about) me." Again, in this case, either sentence could be correct in a given context. The grammar dictates the meaning.

In the following sentences, which is correct?

She tabulates more calls than we.
She tabulates more calls than us.

You're right again: "She tabulates more calls than we (do)." Of these last two sentences, only the first is correct. The second sentence can mean only "She tabulates more calls than she tabulates us"—nonsensical.

If in doubt about this particular construction, go ahead and say the missing word or two aloud either after or before the *than*, and the correct pronoun will become apparent.

▼

MEMORY TIP

Repeat this rhyme: Before or after *than*, under*stand* that there's a *span* of missing words.

27

"You Know What They Always Say About That"

UNCLEAR REFERENCES

"It all started when they wouldn't leave us alone." Who's *they*? When *what* all started? Have you ever wanted to interrupt a storyteller with such questions?

Unclear:

> Surveys, comment cards, and hotlines are popular ways to gather customer satisfaction data. *This* has been the key ingredient in our success.

What does *this* in the previous sentence refer to? Gathering data? Customer satisfaction? Steer clear of sentences containing unclear pronouns; that is, pronouns that can have multiple meanings in the context of a sentence.

> Horatio asked me to design a multifaceted marketing campaign to introduce the new e-book to the marketplace, particularly to the software analysts who already are acquainted with our products and who would be the most likely of our clients to be

interested in them. It should be quick and easy to access. Our team should be able to demo them from anywhere. Then we need to have a way to measure results from it. Are the assumptions and principles we've outlined working? They'll want a way to report their opinions to us.

As you read this previous passage, you may not have been confused at all. That's why this silly error becomes so serious: people don't realize that they've misunderstood what you said until somebody starts asking questions or taking action. To demonstrate what I mean, here's the same passage repeated with my questions inserted beside each unclear reference:

> Horatio asked me to design a multifaceted marketing campaign to introduce the new e-book to the marketplace, particularly to the software analysts who already are acquainted with our products and who would be the most likely of our clients to be interested in *them*. (interested in our products or in the new e-book?)
>
> It should be quick and easy to access. (must be referring to the new e-book, because *it* is singular.)
>
> Our team should be able to demo them from anywhere. (products or e-book? *Them* is plural.)
>
> Then we need to have a way to measure results from it. (results from the marketing campaign or the strategies from the e-book?)
>
> Are the assumptions and principles we've outlined working? (those in the e-book or those in the campaign?)
>
> They'll want a way to report their opinions to us. (buyers will want to report or the sales team will want to report? Who is *us*—the

people responsible for the marketing campaign or the people responsible for creating the e-book content?)

Take care with *this, that, they, these, those,* or *it* when those words can refer to multiple things. Substitute specific nouns for unclear pronouns. Here's the paragraph again—as *they* always say, the third time's the charm.

Horatio asked me to design a multifaceted marketing campaign to introduce the new e-book to the marketplace, particularly to the software analysts who already are acquainted with our products and who would be the most likely of our clients to be interested in the *e-book*. The *new book* should be quick and easy to access. Our team should be able to demo *it and all our products* from anywhere. Then we need to have a way to measure results from clients who use *the book*. Are the assumptions and principles we've outlined working? *The marketing and sales teams* will want a way to report *buyer* opinions to us.

If there's room for confusion, bring the starring noun back on stage and send the understudy to the shower.

MEMORY TIP

"You know what they always say." Consider that common phrase a reminder that people are asking the same thing about your communication: Who are *they*? What's the *it*? What's the *which*?

28

Which Hunts

THAT VERSUS WHICH

Which of the following two sentences is correct?

> People do not buy products *which* seem overpriced and shabbily packaged.
>
> People do not buy products *that* seem overpriced and shabbily packaged.

You can verify the correct answer for yourself in just a moment. The distinction between these two is not difficult if you keep this one simple test in mind: Does the key point of the sentence change if you remove the *that* or *which* clause? (A clause is a group of related words with a subject and verb.)

If you can remove the clause in question and not change the meaning of the sentence, use a comma and *which* to set it off from the rest of the sentence. If you can't, use *that* without a comma. Simple enough, right?

Circle back to the top of the page and identify the correct sentence. Remove "which seem overpriced and shabbily packaged," and you're left with "People do not buy products." This remaining part definitely makes no sense. The *that* clause is essential to its meaning. So the second sentence is the correct one of the two.

Other Examples:

> Ebeneezer submitted his sales report, which was late as usual. (Just added information—you can omit the *which* clause and not lose the gist of the sentence.)
>
> Mortimer parked his car in front of the building that faces Montgomery Street. (You can't omit the *that* clause, or you'll lose the gist of the sentence. He's telling you which building he parked in front of—the building that faces Montgomery Street.)

Just to cement this in your mind, let's say there's only one building in the entire area. Suppose the writer is telling you that Mortimer parked *in front of* the building, not behind it. Here's how the sentence would be written: "Mortimer parked his car in front of the building, which faces Montgomery Street." Now the *which* clause is simply nonessential information that doesn't distinguish this building from any other.

Memory Tip

Think of *which* clauses as "switch" clauses. The *which* signals the reader that you're switching off track briefly to provide additional, nonessential information. Use a comma to set off this side note.

29

Is Shamu a Who?

PEOPLE *WHO* OR *THAT*?

My brother-in-law grew up in a large family of boys. He tells about how often his mother "called the roll" unintentionally when flustered in the hustle and bustle of cooking, cleaning, and caring for a household of six: "Kevin, . . . Mike, . . . uh, . . . I mean . . . Charles, uh, . . . I mean Casey, . . . oh, well, you know who you are," as she finally gave up on recalling the correct name and sent the unlucky one underfoot to run the errand.

People typically prefer to be called by their names. And when names are unavailable, they at least like to feel human as opposed to inanimate. That's the issue with *who* and *that.*

When referring to people (and animals treated as people, such as Shamu, the whale, and Fluffy, the kitten), use *who* or *that.* When referring to places, ideas, or things, use *that, which,* or *it,* not *who.*

MEMORY TIP

People rule. That means they have choices: *that* or *who.* Inanimate objects have to take the leftovers.

PART 3

Modifier Mishaps

No sooner have you learned new software than here comes Release 2.0. Master that, and then here comes Release 3.0. Software gets upgraded. Houses get remodeled. People gain or lose weight, have plastic surgery, and build or lose muscle mass.

Likewise, sentences may start out simple. But then their meanings become modified by added words.

Rufus walked toward the lake.

Rufus walked slowly toward the lake.

Rufus walked very slowly toward the lake.

Alone, Rufus walked very slowly toward the lake.

Alone and dejected, Rufus walked very slowly toward the lake.

Alone and dejected, Rufus walked very slowly toward the lake that rippled gently against the muddy bank.

Alone and dejected—as if he'd lost his best friend—Rufus walked very slowly toward the lake that rippled gently against the muddy bank.

A *modifier* is the term we give to words, phrases, or clauses that "attach to" or describe something, changing (expanding or limiting) its meaning. But as with software modifications, sometimes the modifiers added to sentences cause problems—as explained in the following chapters.

30

Misplaced Modifiers That Mystify

Putting Them in Their Place

When modifiers land in the spot closest to what they describe, the sentence informs and clarifies. When modifiers land out of place, the sentence can confuse or amuse readers.

Incorrect:

At the age of 100, Kilpatrick has been begging his dad to give up driving the car. (This situation has to be a public safety hazard. If Kilpatrick is 100, his dad certainly has to be approaching 120, with failing eyesight and slow reflexes.)

Correct:

Kilpatrick has been begging his dad, at the age of 100, to give up driving his car.

Incorrect:

Injected directly into the lips, the doctor can strengthen the facial muscles with this medication. (The doctor was injected into the lips? A close bedside manner, don't you think?)

Correct:

> Injected directly into the lips, this medication can strengthen the facial muscles.

Incorrect:

> Mislabeled and misfiled, the executives had not read the report. (Were the executives mislabeled and misfiled?)

Correct:

> The executives had not read the mislabeled and misfiled report.

Incorrect:

> Harrison attended the meeting, where he planned to announce the merger with misgivings. (Did the merger have misgivings?)

Correct:

> With misgivings, Harrison attended the meeting, where he planned to announce the merger.

Misplaced adverbs are common culprits. They get dropped in before the verb when they should go after it—or after when they should go before it. Moving one word around can make a big difference. The single-word adverb modifiers most frequently misplaced are these: *almost, only, definitely, often,* and *completely.*

> Trixy only leased this car for her company's sales team. (She only leased the car—she didn't buy it.)
> Trixy leased only this car for her company's sales team. (She leased only one car.)

Trixy leased this car only for her company's sales team. (Only the sales team can use it.)

Trixy leased this car for her only company's sales team. (She has only one company.)

Trixy leased this car for her company's only sales team. (That sales team had better be good.)

My point: slide the adverb around, and double-check your meaning. Example: "This suit *only costs* $638 today?" Or, "This suit *costs only* $638 today?"

MEMORY TIP

Modifiers can mystify. Remember to put them in their place!

Can You Hook Me Up?

DANGLING MODIFIERS

Bob Murphey, a motivational-speaker friend of mine now deceased, lost his arm early in life and made a career of telling funny stories about weird comments people made to him about the situation. He got one of the biggest laughs telling about the time a wide-eyed stranger walked up to him and said, "Mister, did you know you lost your arm there?"

"Yep," Bob deadpanned, "I noticed that."

Silence. No further explanation—to the stranger or Bob's audiences.

Danglers remind me of that conversation. The writer or speaker starts to reveal something. The moment is pregnant, ripe for full revelation, then nothing. Zippo. The next idea just doesn't connect. The words with promise just hang in midair, not connecting to what follows.

> Seeing that no one was injured in the accident, the car was left on the side of the road overnight. (So the car has eyesight? Or did the car's driver see that no one was injured and leave the car on the side of the road? Or, maybe a police officer saw the accident, discovered that no one was injured, and then left the car without stopping to investigate because she was racing to rescue someone from an abduction on the other side of the city. You never know in a case like this.)

That's often the problem with danglers. The writer thinks the meaning is obvious; to the reader, it is not. Such words or phrases dangle because they aren't attached to anything. With misplaced modifiers, at least the words they describe are somewhere in the sentence. But danglers don't attach to anything but a mysterious thought in the speaker's or writer's mind.

> Tired and grouchy, the TV was a comfort each evening after work. (The TV was tired and grouchy?)

More often than not, danglers are verb forms ending in *–ing* or *–ed* (technically called participles). They may dangle at the beginning or the end of a sentence.

> Walking the dog in the quiet before dawn, my cell phone startled me. (Cell phones do have new features today, but I haven't seen the "walking the dog" option on mine yet.)
> Having received approval on the deal earlier in the week, the documents were ready to be signed. (Who received the approval? Where did this wheeler-dealer go? He's not in the sentence anywhere.)

Such sentences jump off the page—when someone else writes them. But they're not as easy to spot in your own writing. The trick to catching them is diligence in looking for those descriptors ending in *–ing* and *–ed*.

Incorrect:
> Downgraded to a category 3 hurricane, Eldora decided to go see her parents over the weekend about her anger over the money. (I'm a little confused here. Is Eldora being referred to as a hurricane because of her temper?)

Correct:

> With the hurricane downgraded to a category 3, Eldora decided to go see her parents over the weekend about her anger over the money.

Incorrect:

> To be as up front as possible about past involvement with that organization, the report contains all employment dates and supervisors. (A report can't be "up front." The writer of that report may decide to be forthcoming or deceitful—but the report has no mind of its own.)

Correct:

> To be as up front as possible about past involvement with that organization, Gertrude listed all employment dates and supervisors in the report.

Incorrect:

> The house should be put on the market immediately, considering my cash-flow situation. (Who is considering the cash-flow situation? The homeowner? The mortgage holder? His creditors? Although this dangler comes at the end of the sentence, the reader still doesn't know who's "considering.")

Correct:

> Considering my cash-flow situation, I've decided to put my house on the market immediately.

Instruction manuals also provide a plethora of examples. Attendees in our technical writing workshops, in fact, see them so often that they can't figure out another way to write their procedures. To correct the danglers in procedures, write directly to the person following the instructions.

Incorrect:

When applying pressure, the tube should be upright. (Is the tube going to apply pressure? Probably, a person will.)

Correct:

When applying pressure, you should place the tube upright.

Correct:

When applying pressure, place the tube upright. (The first phrase now attaches to the understood subject of "you.")

Incorrect:

Using the new code, files should be named by date. (The files probably aren't going to use the codes.)

Correct:

Using the new code, name the files by date.

If you let your descriptors dangle in public, you'll confuse and amuse.

Absolutes: These Common Phrases Don't Dangle

Some common sentence starters seem to dangle—but don't. That is, they don't dangle in the sense we're talking about here. The grammatical term for them is absolutes; they have absolutely nothing to do with the rest of the sentence. Commonly used to introduce a thought, they have become simply manners of speech. You will be perfectly correct to begin a sentence with them. For example: *Generally speaking, international travel is still quite safe on that airline. Granted, the weather is unpredictable this time of year.*

Generally speaking	To tell the truth
Granted	To be perfectly honest
To be sure	To be perfectly clear
Alternatively	Strictly speaking
By and large	In the final analysis
Barring unforeseen circumstances	In the long run
When all is said and done	On the whole
Contrary to popular belief	

MEMORY TIP

Visualize a sentence beginning or ending with a descriptive phrase. That phrase tosses out a rope to lasso the first or last word in the main part of the sentence. If there's no anchor post there (a word that makes sense), the rope falls short. The climber can't hang securely to the mountain. The describing phrase doesn't link correctly to the rest of the sentence.

32

"... Which Is What I Always Say ..."

DANGLING *WHICHS*

Blame this common error on multitasking. People have so many things going on that they start a sentence on one topic and finish it on totally different terrain. For example, my colleague just said to me: "I just finished a pile of evaluations. So glad to have those off my desk, *which* reminds me that I am supposed to call Amber and tell her I can't keep our lunch date because I have a client conference call during the noon hour." What's the *which*—did the desk remind him?

Yes, I'm guilty of speaking in this unedited, stream-of-consciousness manner myself on occasion. But we shouldn't write this way, leaving *whichs* rippling behind us for the reader to wade through.

Which has to substitute for a specific noun in the sentence. It can't refer to a general concept hidden in the reader's mind: "I've been sick, which reminds me: I need to have my prescription refilled." Yes, we understand that the writer probably means the fact that she's been sick reminds her. But *which* must refer to a specific noun—and no noun in this sentence logically connects to the *which*.

Does the following ramble sound similar to some you've heard?

I was planning to drive to Denver to visit my family last week-end, which is always a riot because you never know what'll happen. (*What's always a riot—Denver? The family? Weekends?*) And so I ran into this guy that I used to date off and on a couple of years ago when I pulled into a service station for gas. We chatted a few minutes and decided to get a bite to eat at a nearby restaurant, which is something I don't typically do. (*Chat? Eat? Interrupt a planned trip? Date an old boyfriend?*) He spent the first half hour talking about himself, only stopping to order day-old spaghetti, which is why I stopped dating him in the first place! (*Because he ordered spaghetti? Because he talked about himself incessantly?*)

Rid yourself of this bad habit before it sends your friends and family to an early grave.

MEMORY TIP

*Which*s must stand for something, or readers will mistake them for everything.

33

Troublesome Twosomes

ONE WORD OR TWO?

The following pairs of words commonly create confusion. Most of these pairs (though not all) contain an adverb that tells more about the verb—how, where, when, why, or to what degree.

a lot (*many, much:* Pongo likes Chinese food a lot.)
alot (*nonstandard*)

all right (*sufficient, appropriate:* The invoice seems to be all right.)
alright (*nonstandard*)

all together (*all things in the same place, simultaneously, collectively:* The team was all together when I mentioned the problem.)
altogether (*totally, entirely:* The report is altogether too much trouble at this late date.)

all ready (*fully prepared:* She was all ready for the interview.)
already (*previously:* She already knew the answers before they asked the questions.)

any more (*additionally:* She doesn't have any more friends.)
anymore (*any longer:* He doesn't love me anymore.)

any one (*emphasizing one person as opposed to others in a group*: Any one of the CEO's golfing buddies could have told you the truth.)

anyone (*generic meaning of anybody or all*: Anyone can win this award if he or she works hard enough.)

any way (*any method*: I didn't have any way to call because I forgot my phone.)

anyway (*Use this word of the pair in all other situations. Technically, it's an adverb, meaning nevertheless, in any case, or regardless*: I never thought to call, but I didn't have a phone anyway.)

every day (*daily, day by day*: He phones every day.)

everyday (*descriptive word, used before a noun*: I carry my everyday handbag and jewelry when I travel internationally.)

every one (*emphasizing one person as opposed to others in a group*: Every one of the members of the team expects a raise.)

everyone (*generic meaning of everybody or all*: Everyone can expect a raise if the team does well.)

may be (*part of the verb is; also can be helping words in other action verbs*: Hortense may be sick tomorrow, and she may be traveling.)

maybe (*adverb meaning possibly*: Maybe I am wrong.)

some time (*a period of time; a descriptive word plus a noun*: Mortimer has some time available at the end of the week.)

sometime (*an adverb referring to when*: Mortimer invited me to stop by and see him sometime; he said he was sure he had some time available this month.)

To select the correct word, create variations of the thought in the same context. If the variations require two words, the correct choice in your original sentence will become clear.

Example:
Spike doesn't want to hire (*anymore* or *any more?*) auditors.

Variation:
Spike doesn't want to hire three more auditors.

In this variation, *three* and *more* are clearly two separate words. Conclusion: *Any* and *more* have to be two separate words in the same context. So:

Correct:
Spike doesn't want to hire any more auditors.

Another Example:
Jamale didn't know anyone at the conference, but she attended (*any way* or anyway?).

Variation:
Jamale didn't know anyone at the conference, but she attended several ways.

Conclusion: *Anyway* can't be divided into two words in this context—it doesn't make sense. It's a one-word adverb. So:

Correct:
Jamale didn't know anyone at the conference, but she attended anyway.

MEMORY TIP

Try a variation of the sentence in question. If you're able to change half the "word," your context requires two words.

34

Learn This Backwards and Forwards

THE UNNECESSARY –S

Save the extra –s on these directions: not *backwards, towards, anyways,* or *anywheres.* Correct: *backward, toward, anyway, anywhere.* The extra letter has gone the way of the typewriter, keypunch, slide rule, eight-track, and percolator.

Incorrect:
> The supervisor stepped backwards and fell from the platform.

Correct:
> The supervisor stepped backward and fell from the platform.

Incorrect:
> My boss believes that winning this contract does not matter anyways in the long-term relationship with this client.

Correct:
> My boss believes that winning this contract does not matter anyway in the long-term relationship with this client.

MEMORY TIP

The world has become too crowded for the extraneous—like extra –s's.

35

A Honor or an Honor to Be Here?

THE ARTICLES: A OR AN?

Articles of Incorporation. Articles of Agreement. Articles of Faith. Organizers of people and information like to use the term *articles* as a means to categorize and classify. So as you might expect, grammarians have selected *articles* as a label for the three words that point out nouns: *the*, *a*, and *an*.

▶ Use *a* before words that begin with a consonant.
▶ Use *an* before words that begin with a vowel or vowel sound.

Dilbert hired *a* turkey for *an* assistant.
Ebeneezer created *an* eye-appealing brochure and *a* wall poster.
Pongo won *an* attendance award and *a* sales prize.
Wilmo considers it *an* honor to speak to *an* artisan of your caliber.
    (The *h* in *honor* is silent, so the word begins with a vowel sound.)
Gertrude reports *an* incident like carjacking to *a* dispatcher rather than to her boss.

The *n* in *an* keeps the two vowel sounds distinct (the article *a* and the initial vowel of the following word).

MEMORY TIP

When you need the *n* to separate vowel sounds, imagine yourself enunciating like an opera star.

PART 4

Adjective and Adverb Attitudes

Adjectives tell more about nouns and pronouns. These describing words limit or expand the meaning of the nouns or pronouns they surround. Examples:

The late March report
Those ugly, torn chairs in the lobby
That bulk-volume contract *signed* last week
His manipulative manager *working* in the back office

Adverbs tell more about verbs, adverbs, adjectives, and sometimes the whole sentence.

He resigned *quickly* after they discovered the fraud. (describes the verb *resigned*.)

The competition is *so much* stronger than it was last season. (*So* describes the adverb *much*; *much* describes the adjective *stronger*.)

He found it *very* difficult to do a good job. (describes the adjective *difficult*.)

Frankly, I don't care who wins the contract. (describes the entire sentence.)

Sometimes whether you select the adjective or the adverb form of a word dictates the entire meaning of the sentence—as you'll see in this next section.

36

"She Did Things Different"

ADJECTIVES MODIFYING VERBS—A NO-NO

Pardon my disputing your word, but she didn't—do things *different*, that is. She may have done them *differently*. Most people do things differently, so I wouldn't want to bet against you on that.

Adverbs tell more about verbs (and sometimes about adverbs and adjectives, and occasionally about the whole sentence).

As a reminder, adjectives tell more about nouns and pronouns.

The rosebush grew tall. (*Tall* is an adjective—tells more about the noun *rosebush*.)

The rosebush grew quickly. (*Quickly* is an adverb—tells more about the verb *grew*.)

The manager speaks harshly. (*Harshly* is an adverb—tells more about the verb *speaks*.)

The manager's tone is harsh. (*Harsh* is an adjective—tells more about a noun, *the manager's tone*.)

The employee is productive. (*Productive* is an adjective—tells about the noun *employee*.)

The employee works productively. (*Productively* is an adverb—tells about the verb *works*)

The most common mix-ups happen when adjectives collide with verbs. That is, people mistakenly use the adjective form of a word (leave off the –ly) when they need an adverb.

Incorrect:

This product sells quick when the price is right.

The manager spoke real candid about his ambitions for the future.

Dilbert organized the proposal brilliant for this competitive situation.

He restructured the department careful so as not to upset people.

He invested his money cautious.

The following sentences are correct, with adverbs describing the verbs:

Correct:

The product sells *quickly* when the price is right. (how it sells)

The manager spoke real *candidly* about his ambitions for the future. (how he spoke)

Percival organized the proposal *brilliantly* for this competitive situation. (how he organized)

Pongo restructured the department *carefully* so as not to upset people. (how he restructured)

He invested his money *cautiously*. (how he invested)

The manager *is* candid, but she *speaks* candidly. The proposal may *be* brilliant, but it's *organized* brilliantly. Pongo may *have been* careful, but he *restructured* carefully. The difference comes down to what you're describing—the person/thing or the action.

Add –ly on descriptors telling more about the verb, and you'll solve 95 percent of the adverb errors. *Run quickly. Approve knowingly.*

Engaged single-handedly. Negotiated confidently. Judged fairly. Reported objectively. Chatted aimlessly. Pushed relentlessly. Managed faithfully. Fired fearlessly. Hired enthusiastically. Scored triumphantly.

MEMORY TIP

If the descriptor refers to the action (verb) rather than the person/thing, add the –*ly*.

37

"The Team Played Real Good"

WELL VERSUS GOOD

I don't mean to argue again here, but they didn't. The team may have played *well*. But it didn't play *good*. I bet you're wondering how I know when I wasn't even at the game, right?

Good describes something or somebody. (Like other adjectives, *good* can be used to describe only nouns or pronouns—people, places, things, or ideas.) Examples:

Mortimer is a good manager.
Florida is a good location for our warehouse.
Those engineers made a good decision in drilling for oil.
Freedom from pricing restrictions is a good idea.

Well tells how something is done. Examples:

Dilbert writes well.
The engineering team planned well.
The machines run well.
The car drives well in most road conditions.

In any given situation, ask yourself: Am I talking about a thing, person, place, or idea? If so, use *good*. Or, am I talking about how something or somebody performed? If so, use *well*.

▼

MEMORY TIP

An advertisement for an optometry clinic appeared in the *Houston Chronicle*. The caption above the photo of a beautiful girl wearing eyeglasses read: "The frames make you look good; we make you look well."

Good is correct because it refers to the person (you).
Well is correct because it refers to how you look (meaning "see").

The caption meant this: The frames make you as a person look beautiful or handsome. Our optometrists make you see well.

Obviously, the company hired a clever grammarian as its marketing agent. Readers probably puzzled over that ad for a day or two before they "caught" the meaning. And if you're writing advertising copy, that's the idea—to catch people's attention.

You, of course, will no longer be puzzled by such clever ads.

Not only do you look *good*, but also you understand the difference *well*.

38

"This Job Is More Simpler Than What I Had Before"

COMPARING WITH MORE AND MOST

If you have siblings, you probably don't like to be compared. Those comparisons can be especially troublesome when done by teachers: "Pudge, you're not as good a math student as your sister, Jamale, was. She was always brighter, faster, and more conscientious than you in doing her homework." No, indeed, that's not a pleasant remark and reminder.

But deal with it, and let's focus on the language. Why the choice of *brighter* and *faster* when the teacher compared Pudge and Jamale? And then the switch to *more conscientious*? Why not *conscientiouser*? Sure it's a tongue twister, but why not *positiver* about doing her homework? Or *pleasanter* about doing her homework?

When using a one-syllable word to compare things or people, you typically add *–er* or *–est: quick, quicker, quickest; sharp, sharper, sharpest; limp, limper, limpest; sick, sicker, sickest; light, lighter, lightest; heavy, heavier, heaviest; rainy, rainier, rainiest.*

But when using longer adjectives (words of two or more syllables) to compare things or people, you typically need the help of *more* or *less*, *most* or *least*: *more brilliant, most brilliant; more flavorful, most flavorful; more confusing, most confusing; more explicit, most explicit; less miserable, least miserable; less memorable, least memorable; less understandable, least understandable.*

Some adjectives used to compare people or things are totally different words altogether:

My steak is *good*. Winnifred's steak is *better*. Spike's steak is the *best*.
Pongo is *ill*. Ebeneezer is *worse*. Eldora is the *worst*.
Percival drinks far too *many* sodas. Pongo drinks even *more* sodas.
Ebeneezer drinks the *most* sodas of all three.

MEMORY TIP

Comparing is as simple as counting 1, 2.

If the adjective has only one syllable, add one syllable to compare (*–er, –est*).

If the adjective already has two or more syllables, leave it alone. Instead, add a word to compare (*more* or *most*; *less* or *least*).

39

"It's the Most Unique Gift I've Ever Received!"

UNIQUE, ROUND, SQUARE, SURROUNDED, PERFECT—OR NOT?

Either something is unique or it isn't. Either something is round, or it's squashed, deflated, oval, or some other oddity—but not round. Either something is square—or it was built by the guy who built my last house. Either it's perfect, flat, surrounded—or not. There's no "in between" state. To insist that something is *more unique, more perfect, almost surrounded,* or the *most square* of the group shows a misunderstanding of the original word.

MEMORY TIP

Think in terms of black or white, not shades of gray. With the words *round, square, flat, unique, perfect,* and *surrounded,* consider the old song lyrics: "There's No Mr. In-Between."

40

"This Checkout—20 Items or Less"

LESS VERSUS FEWER

No matter which grocery checkout aisle is under discussion, the people in line don't have 20 items or less. That's not because you picked the wrong lane again. It's just a point of grammar. If you can count the items, the people have *fewer* or *more*, not less. If the nature of any item makes it impossible to count, refer to it with the words *less* and *more*.

Example:

I have *less time* than I used to, *less inclination* to do what I don't want to do, and *less willpower* to put up with poor customer service when traveling. But I get *fewer opportunities* than ever to kick back and take long vacations. In fact, *fewer workers* in all industries take their full vacations these days because of heavy workloads. Maybe if *fewer employers* were willing to give up personal time to check their BlackBerries, iPhones, or Treos hourly to stay in touch with the office, then there would be *less stress* and *more peace* around the place. Then when people returned to work, *fewer hours* would be wasted on nonproductive activities.

Reverse this logic to remember it: That is, you'd never say, "I have *fewer help* today than I'm going to need to finish my project." "Pongo has *fewer experience* in management than he needs to be considered for this promotion." "You have given *fewer attention* to these skills than is required to do a good job."

So if you don't use *fewer* with singular words like *help, experience,* or *attention,* neither do you use *less* with plural words like *employees, hours,* or *cars.*

MEMORY TIP

If you can count it, use *fewer.* If not, use *less.*

41

"He Has Over a Million Miles on That Airline"

OVER VERSUS MORE THAN

The passenger would probably be far safer riding *inside* the plane. The confusion between *over* and *more than* is understandable. *Over* refers to a physical position. *More than* applies to amounts. The two words are synonyms, but not interchangeable.

Incorrect:
Gertrude has over 10 years of military experience.

Correct:
Gertrude has more than 10 years of military experience.

Correct:
Ebeneezer has more than a million excuses for why he can't get his reports finished on time.
Mortimer went over his boss's head to ask for a raise.

Fritz looked over the blueprints and explained the changes.

Wilmo has more than four different supervisors who rate his work.

Eldora wants to be paid double time for more than 40 hours.

▼

MEMORY TIP

Imagine that your friend is a contestant on a TV game show and that you're watching from the studio audience, which is allowed to help contestants onstage. The host asks your friend a question: "How many unemployed heads of household, with four children, live in the state of New York?"

Your friend starts to guess aloud before giving a final answer to the show's host. Trying to help your friend, you shout out, "More."

Your friend guesses a higher number.

You shout, "More."

Your friend guesses still higher.

"More."

Final guess. The game show host reveals the answer. Your friend wins, thanks to your help. The game ends.

Instant replay:

Would you ever say to your friend, "Over that." "No, over that." "No, over that."

Probably not.

When you're talking about numbers, the correct phrase is *higher* or *more than*, not *over* (unless, of course, you're talking about fences).

42

"I Like Smaller Cars"

INCOMPLETE COMPARISONS

Do people who talk in circles drive you crazy? The only person less maddening than someone talking in circles is someone talking in half-circles.

Case in Point:
> Daffy likes the Midwest better. (What two areas of the country are being compared? Better than what? Better than she used to like the Midwest? Better than she likes the Northeast? Better than Fritz likes the Midwest?)

Correct:
Daffy likes the Midwest better than the South.

Half the comparison is stated, but the second half of the comparison is only in the speaker's head.

Want to drive your friends and family nuts? Try a few of the following:

Incorrect:
> This is a longer report. (Longer than what? Longer than I expected? Longer than the one sent last year? Longer than the

one other vendors send? Longer that the one someone else wrote?)

Correct:

This report is longer than what I expected.

Incorrect:

May's sales are higher than April. (Really? Then April had better work harder, because May is outselling her. Probably, the speaker is referring to months rather than women.)

Correct:

Sales in May are higher than sales were in April.

Incorrect:

For months, I've been interviewing general contractors about a new office building, and I've finally found someone who seems more dependable and trustworthy. (Than who? Than most builders? Than a past builder used? Than the builder interviewed last week?)

Correct:

For months, I've been interviewing general contractors about a new office building, and I've finally found someone who seems more dependable and trustworthy than the contractor who built my last office complex.

Incorrect:

Rufus dislikes consultants more than his boss. (Does Rufus dislike consultants more than he dislikes his boss? Or, does Rufus dislike consultants more than his boss dislikes consultants?)

Correct:

Well, your choice—maybe you know Rufus.

Incorrect:

Mortimer saw Eldora give a presentation last week; he said she had much more confidence. (Than what or who?)

Correct:

Mortimer saw Eldora give a presentation last week; he said she had much more confidence than previously.

Incorrect:

Fourth-quarter sales are higher than third quarter. (The sales are higher than the third quarter? Really? Now that you understand this error, it's starting to sound silly to you, isn't it?)

Correct:

The fourth-quarter sales are higher than the third-quarter sales.

When comparing things, talk in circles and "finish the loop." Longer than what? Different from what? Taller than who? Bigger than what? Older than who? More expensive than what?

MEMORY TIP

Imagine the listener or reader raising an eyebrow and asking: as compared to what? As compared to who? As compared to when?

PART 5

Parallel Bars and Balance Beams

Clothing consultants charge big bucks to help clients update their current wardrobes with the season's newest fashions—shoes with handbags, jewelry with dresses and pantsuits, ties with suits. Interior designers do the same thing in helping families select home furnishings—matching lamps on end tables, matching photo frames, coordinating wallpaper and draperies. It should be no surprise, then, that items have to "match" in a grammatically correct sentence.

Parallelism is the grammatical term given to that matching concept.

43

To Balance or Not to Balance—That Is the Question

PARALLELISM PERFECTED

Great orators and philosophers through the centuries have put the power of parallelism to use in these classic lines:

> "A government of the people, by the people, for the people."
> "To be or not to be—that is the question."
> "Ask not what your country can do for you; ask what you can do for your country."
> "If I loved you less, I might be able to talk about it more."
> "Better to reign in Hell than serve in Heaven."
> "It's not *what* you know; it's *who* you know."
> "Fish or cut bait."

Well, okay, maybe not all of these are classics, but you get my drift.

Equal ideas have to match or balance in the way you express them. That is, they all should be verbs, nouns, complete sentences, only phrases, and so forth.

Equal ideas deserve similar structure and expression.

Incorrect:

You can either pay now or you can pay later. (*Pay now* and *pay later* are the equivalent ideas that need to balance. So the *either/or* should link them together in exactly the same way.)

Correct:

You can either pay now or pay later.

Incorrect:

He doesn't know whether renting more office space or to try to hire a virtual sales team would be the better approach. (*Renting more office space* and *trying to hire a virtual sales team* are the equivalent ideas that need to balance. So the *whether/or* should link them together in matching expressions.)

Correct:

He doesn't know whether renting more office space or trying to hire a virtual sales team would be the better approach.

MEMORY TIP

Para . . . llel sounds like *pair*. A pair of ideas should be expressed (or dressed) as twins.

44

"I Worked, Waited, and Was Rewarded"

PARALLELISM WITH A VIEWPOINT CHANGE

Politicians can change their viewpoints on issues from decade to decade, or even from day to day, for that matter. But you can't.

Incorrect:

> Taxes on small businesses passed from parents to their children have become outrageous, and you shouldn't have to pay them.

Do you see the problem with the previous statement? The writer starts out talking about small businesses in general (third-person viewpoint), and then switches in mid-sentence to talk to "you," the reader, directly (second-person viewpoint).

This chart presents the three viewpoints:

First person	I, we, our, my (including yourself in the statement)	"I completed this form."
Second person	you (addressing another person directly—the "you" may be understood as with a command)	"Complete this form." Or: "You need to complete this form."
Third person	he, she, they, freedom, clients (talking about someone or something but not addressing them directly and not including yourself in the statement)	"They completed this form."

With the incorrect sentence given earlier, you can change either the first part or the second part to make the viewpoint consistent:

Correct:

Taxes on small businesses passed from parents to their children have become outrageous, and business owners shouldn't have to pay them.

Your taxes on a small business passed down from your parents have become outrageous. You shouldn't have to pay them.

Incorrect:

All vendors should e-mail their invoices, and please attach copies of the work orders.

Correct:

Please e-mail your invoices, and attach copies of the work orders. All vendors should e-mail their invoices and attach copies of the work orders.

Incorrect:

The clinic will see patients beginning at 2:00; you'll also need to bring proof of insurance.

Correct:

The clinic will see patients beginning at 2:00; the clinic staff will also need to see patients' proof of insurance coverage.
You can schedule an appointment at the clinic or drop by after it opens at 2:00. You'll also need to bring proof of insurance coverage.

Incorrect:

You must schedule weekly staff meetings, and managers also need to participate in regional meetings during the last week of each month.

Correct:

Managers must schedule weekly staff meetings, and they'll need to participate in regional meetings during the last week of each month.
You must schedule weekly staff meetings and participate in regional meetings during the last week of each month.

Of course, if you write or speak more than one sentence, you're probably going to change viewpoints several times. No one will complain about that unless the changes are needless and confusing.

But in general, make up your mind. Either talk *to* people (*you*) or *about* them (*he, they, houses, clients, zoos, cars, bazookas*) or *about* yourself (*I, we*) within a sentence.

MEMORY TIP

Visualize a political "attack" ad that shows clips of the candidate switching his or her viewpoint on an issue. Don't follow suit. Be consistent.

45

Verbs With Attitude

Active and Passive Voice

Suppose you are CEO and your VP of sales says to you, "The prospect rejected our proposal, and you may also be surprised to discover that our name has been removed from the bidders list." You'll probably be wondering who removed your name from the client's bidders list.

The sentence doesn't provide the information. And therein lies the problem with passive voice. Does your VP have "an attitude" and just not want to be forthcoming with the information? Is the VP protecting someone? Or is she just a careless communicator?

Let's analyze:

If the subject of the sentence acts, the verb is active. If the subject of the sentence receives action, the verb is passive.

Active:

> Spike hires a new salesperson each month. (The subject *Spike* acts.)

Passive:

> A new salesperson is hired each month. (The subject *salesperson* receives action—gets hired.)

Active:

Judd wrote the e-mail. (The subject *Judd* acts.)

Passive:

The e-mail was written by Judd. (The subject *e-mail* receives action—Judd wrote it.)

Active:

The market is plunging today. (The subject *market* acts.)

Passive:

The market was flooded by traders dumping stocks. (The subject *market* receives action—it got flooded.)

Active:

Pay the fare online. (The understood subject *you* should act.)

Passive:

The fare should be paid online. (Somebody should do something to the subject *fare*—pay it.)

Active-voice verbs generally make writing crisp, clear, and concise. Passive-voice verbs also have a place and purpose: they add variety, slow the pace, and focus on the results and action of the sentence if the doer is unimportant.

The grammar goof happens when the two (both active and passive verbs) are mixed in one sentence or, worse, within one clause, creating inconsistency and confusion about who's doing what. Back to the earlier situation: "The prospect rejected (active) our proposal, and you may also be (active) surprised to discover that our name has been removed (passive) from the client's bidders list."

Passive-voice verbs often remove the doers or actors altogether from the sentence drama. The feel is much like a theater with a voice-over and no characters visible on the set. Generally, who does what is important. That's why the passive voice often leads to clarity problems.

Passive:

> The winner of the award has already been selected. (by whom?)
> The negotiated deal has been rejected. (by which side?)
> The decision was made to move ahead with the project. (by whom?)
> The problem is being escalated to the CEO. (by whom?)
> The contract has been signed by the client. (doer included here)

Active:

> The prospect rejected our proposal, and the *evaluation team* removed our name from the client's bidders list.

Even if you don't care who does what in any given situation, make all verbs within a sentence either consistently active or consistently passive.

Incorrect:

> You need to sign these checks, and the social security number should be written on them.

Correct:

> You need to sign these checks and write your social security number on them.

Incorrect:

Phones will be installed in every office, and they will repaint walls. (Phones will repaint the walls?)

Correct:

Phones will be installed in every office, and the walls will be repainted.

The night crew will install phones in every office and repaint the walls.

Don't create mysteries when you write. Unless you need the passive voice for a specific purpose, put actors on stage in your sentences.

MEMORY TIP

Use active or passive verbs consistently within a sentence. And as a rule of thumb, put people in your prose (active voice) for clear, concise writing.

46

Time Marches On—
But at the Same Pace

DON'T BE LAX ABOUT TENSE CHANGES

Granted, anyone knows that two weeks on a diet passes more slowly than two weeks on a vacation. But technically speaking, two weeks is two weeks. So if you're talking about the present time frame, keep all the verbs in the present tense. If you're talking about something that happened in the past, keep all the verbs in the past tense. Flip-flopping between tenses confuses people. Here's an example.

Mixed Tenses:

We *have been trying* to hire a marketing director for several months. Having checked résumés from several online sources, we *have been* disappointed in the candidates that we *have chosen* to interview. Several candidates *hype* their experience but *do* not *bring* portfolios of their work. Many *do* not *want* us to contact previous supervisors. We *contacted* recruiters about helping us to fill the position for a fee of 25 percent. Some *have estimated* that it *may take* up to three to six months to fill the

position with the right person. We *have set* a target date of June
1 to have the position filled.

Question: Is this manager currently using a recruiter to fill the
position? That's unclear because of the unnecessary tense change here:
"We contacted recruiters about helping us to fill the position for a fee
of 25 percent." (Past tense—an action that's over and done with, com-
pleted, terminado, finito.) Yet all the other verbs in the paragraph are
present perfect tense (the time frame describing actions begun in the
past and still ongoing in the present).

That one odd tense change creates the confusion.

Consistent:

We *have been trying* to hire a marketing director for several
months. Having checked résumés from several online sources,
we *have been* disappointed in the candidates that we *have chosen* to interview. Several candidates *hype* their experience but
do not *bring* portfolios of their work. Many *do* not *want* us to
contact previous supervisors. We *have contacted* recruiters
about helping us to fill the position for a fee of 25 percent.
Some *have estimated* that it *may take* up to three to six months
to fill the position with the right person. We *have set* a target
date of June 1 to have the position filled.

With the verb tense consistent, it's clear that they are still con-
tacting recruiters and considering their help.

If you're talking about different time periods, by all means, you'll
need to switch tenses:

Pudge bought (*past*) a new Mercedes yesterday and had (*past*) a wreck in it this morning. The tow truck is pulling (*present*) the car into the repair shop now. Pudge plans (*present*) to babysit the car at the body shop until they repaint (*present*) it. He will not return (*future*) to work until Friday.

If you have reason to change tenses, do so. If not, don't.

MEMORY TIP

As poet and philosopher Henry David Thoreau put it, "If a man does not keep pace with his companions, perhaps it is because he hears a different drummer." Just make sure your drummer can keep a consistent beat.

PART 6

Punctuation Problems

Consider the difference punctuation makes in the two letters penned by Richard Lederer and John Shore in their book *Com ı Sense: A Fun-damental Guide to Punctuation* (St. Martin's Press, 20(`.

My Dear Pat,

The dinner we shared the other night—it was absolutely lovely! Not in my wildest dreams could I ever imagine anyone as perfect as you are. Could you—if only for a moment—think of our being together forever? What a cruel joke to have you come into my life only to leave again; it would be heaven denied. The possibility of seeing you again makes me giddy with joy. I face the time we are apart with great sadness.

John

P.S. I would like to tell you that I love you. I can't stop thinking that you are one of the prettiest women on earth.

My Dear,

Pat the dinner we shared the other night. It was absolutely lovely—not! In my wildest dreams, could I ever imagine anyone? As perfect as you are, could you—if only for a moment—think? Of our being together forever: what a cruel joke! To have you come into my life only to leave again: it would be heaven! Denied the possibility of seeing you again makes me giddy. With joy I face the time we are apart.

With great "sadness,"

John

P.S. I would like to tell you that I love you. I can't. Stop thinking that you are one of the prettiest women on earth.

One letter may lead to marriage; the other, to assault.

On the other hand, proper punctuation puts power in your prose. Let me defer to Ben Franklin on this point. He summed it up well in his *Almanac* of 1757:

For want of a nail the shoe was lost,
For want of a shoe the horse was lost,
For want of a horse the rider was lost,
For want of a rider the battle was lost,
For want of a battle the Kingdom was lost,
And all for the want of a horseshoe nail.

Likewise, customers and contracts can be won or lost for lack of a comma or hyphen. If you want to confuse your readers, consider these sentences: "Bruno insisted Millie hacked into the computer system" Or: "Bruno, insisted Millie, hacked into the computer system." The commas determine who's going to prison.

Or, pity the poor person trying to follow these instructions: "Turn the knob and depress the button on the shaft. Take care that you do not cause an explosion at this point." Does this mean that turning the knob depresses the button? Or is the button a second action step? If they're two steps, do you do them simultaneously or one after the other? So if you get things wrong, an explosion will let you know? Great warning system.

Someone mailed me the following caption from a newspaper clipping: "O. J. Simpson said his lawyer was sad and depressed." But with the kinds of fees lawyers charge, why would the lawyers be so depressed? This version is probably what the caption writer intended: "O. J. Simpson, said his lawyer, was sad and depressed."

To put it pointedly: Scattering punctuation marks incoherently throughout a document changes the meaning of what you write.

(Fortunately, you can't make punctuation errors as you speak. So if you're one of the few people on the planet who never write e-mails, thank-you notes, reports, or proposals, you can skip this punctuation section with permission.)

47

Comma Hiccups

Have you ever tried to talk with someone who had the hiccups? The condition tends to slow the conversation. Likewise, when someone unexpectedly tosses extra commas into a sentence, the reading pace slows dramatically. A paragraph begins to looks like this:

> Those people, working in my areas, across from the main lobby and visitor parking lots, cannot attend the morning sessions. They need to attend, in the afternoon, or after their normal workday. An outside instructor, specializing in performance feedback, will be presenting these training classes, and he is also available, for personal coaching, in the afternoons, if you would like, to set appointments. His phone number, is 903-555-1232.

Too many commas in your sentence contribute to misreading, amusement, and even irritation. Why irritation? People like to control their own reading pace. Slow them with commas only for clarity or other good reasons. And never trick them by tossing in an inappropriate comma that changes the meaning of the sentence altogether. (More about that later.)

Wrong places to slow a reader with an unnecessary comma:

▶ Between a descriptive word and the noun it describes

Incorrect:
She bought a few run-down, inexpensive, houses to remodel.

Correct:
She bought a few run-down, inexpensive houses to remodel.

▶ Between a subject and a verb

Incorrect:
Growing the company through acquisitions, has been a challenge.

Correct:
Growing the company through acquisitions has been a challenge.

▶ Between two phrases joined by a conjunction

Incorrect:
Bruno was hired in August, but was fired almost immediately.

Correct:
Bruno was hired in August but was fired almost immediately.
Bruno was hired in August, but *he* was fired almost immediately.

MEMORY TIP

If you can't give a specific reason for a comma, don't cause a hiccup in the flow of thoughts.

Comma Clauses and Pauses

What people do intuitively with their voice inflection often bewilders them in writing. The challenge is translating voice inflection to the page.

To be more dramatic about it: cut a comma, and you may destroy someone's career.

To repeat: a comma tells a reader to pause. The absence of a comma means that a reader should keep going full speed ahead. If you set off the middle or final part of a sentence with a comma, you're telling a reader that part is nonessential—that it adds information but is not essential to the meaning of the sentence.

If you can't remove that part of the sentence without changing the meaning of what's left, then don't set that part off with commas.

Let's try it: "Pudge prefers to work with clients who have multiyear contracts."

Question: Do you need a comma to set off the *who* clause? Well, try the rule: Omit the final part to verify that it's nonessential and that what's left of the sentence has the same meaning: "Pudge prefers to work with clients." That remaining part has a different meaning. Pudge doesn't prefer just any clients; he's particular. He prefers clients with multiyear contracts. "Who have multiyear contracts" is essential to the meaning of the sentence. Result: It is incorrect to set that part off with a comma.

Okay, try another example: "Brunhilda submitted our proposal, which has a strong chance of winning, to the European client last week."

Question: Do you need commas around the *which* clause to set it off from the rest of the sentence? Try the rule again: omit that part to verify that it's nonessential and to see if the meaning of the sentence changes without it: "Brunhilda submitted our proposal to the European client last week." The meaning of what remains does not change. Result: These enclosing commas are used correctly; "which has a strong chance of winning" is additional information but nonessential to the meaning of *proposal.*

Consider how you would inflect your voice and where you would pause in the following sentences. (Although I'm not suggesting that you learn to punctuate by voice inflection, that system will help you determine the meaning in your own sentences and understand the use of commas to set off nonessential elements.)

Correct:

I knew the man who bought my car. (Essential: the *who* clause tells which man—no comma.)

Daffy signed the contract, which the client mailed overnight. (Nonessential: the *which* clause just adds information about the contract but doesn't distinguish this contract from another—comma to set off.)

According to this contract, which I've not seen until this morning, we have 30 days to pay the invoice. (Nonessential: the *which* clause just adds extra information about the contract but does not distinguish it from other contracts—commas to set off.)

The emcee explained the agenda that the panel would follow during the second session. (Essential: the *that* clause tells which agenda—no commas to set it off.)

Here's a rule of thumb for those essential and nonessential clauses that involve *that* and *which:*

▶ *Which* clauses give nonessential information. Use commas to set them off.

▶ *That* clauses provide essential information. Don't use a comma.

MEMORY TIP

Remember the "I think that . . . blah, blah, blah" model sentence.

You'd never consider it a complete idea to write or say only "*I think.*" Instead, you typically tell someone *what* you think. You think it's too hot. You think you deserve a raise. You think Congress needs to cut taxes. The *that* part is essential to your "I think" sentence. A model *that* clause introduces essential information and needs no comma.

"Hi Hank, What Do You Think Frank?"

COMMAS WHEN ADDRESSING PEOPLE DIRECTLY

Eons ago, when people wrote each other letters, they began "Darling Brunhilda," "Dear Bruno," "My dear Hannah," or "Dear Mr. Hartford," whether they intended to invite the recipient for dinner or a duel.

E-mail has changed our format and tone. Often the salutation is "Hi, Fritz." No problem—as long as the writer remembers that *Hi* isn't an equivalent for *Dear*. *Dear* is an adjective—a descriptive word (unless, of course, you're calling someone Dear as a name instead of Honey Buns or Hot Lips). *Hi* is a greeting. Big difference.

When you write

Dear Fritz,

Blah, blah, blah . . .

you add only the comma after the name. You are describing Fritz as someone dear—even though nowadays no one takes the term seriously and you may actually hate Fritz's guts. On the other hand, when you write

Hi, Fritz,

Blah, blah, blah . . .

you are not describing Fritz in any way. You are simply talking to Fritz directly. So you set off Fritz's name as you would in any other situation when directing your comments specifically to a person: "Fritz, may I have a word with you in my office?" "In my opinion, Trixy, you're about to make a big mistake." "Why did you, Pongo, of all people, attend this meeting?" "How did you know where we ate lunch, Eldora?"

The misunderstanding in thinking that those two greetings are the same and therefore should be punctuated the same way spills over into general writing.

Playing therapist now, I'm guessing that the origin of this recent habit is also e-mail greetings: Because e-mail writers have become so accustomed to the contagiously incorrect "Hi Paul—" opening, they are failing to set off all names of people they're talking to in their sentences:

Incorrect:

Hi Hank.

What do you think Frank?

Trixy is it you that I will be presenting the report to on Friday?

In my opinion Fritz the software is the real problem.

I don't understand Pudge why we weren't given a chance to bid on this project.

Wrong, wrong, wrong. When you're talking to someone, you have to get that person's attention: Set off the name with commas so that the reader pauses before and after, and takes notice that you're speaking directly to him or her.

This habit has gotten way out of control: "Thanks Spike." "See you later Dilbert." "Hey Kilpatrick are you attending the meeting on Thursday?" Without the comma and pause, Spike, Dilbert, and Kilpatrick may doze right through such comments, not realizing that you're talking to them. Instead, look them in the eye, address them directly, and slap them upside the head with that comma to get their attention.

Hi, Hank—
Thanks, Spike!
See you later, Dilbert.
Hey, Kilpatrick, are you attending the meeting on Thursday?

When you talk to people, punctuate so that they'll listen.

MEMORY TIP

When talking to people directly, add the comma, and figuratively pause until they look you in the eye.

50

Dear Spike

PUNCTUATION AFTER SALUTATIONS

Businesspeople have had serious problems with dress on casual Fridays. Bosses complain that some people show up in the proper collared shirt and khakis, while others wander in to work in cut-offs and T-shirts. Apparently, that same confusion between formal and casual dress has spilled over into salutations.

Somehow the formal "Dear Mr. Gonzales:" of letter writing and the informal "Hey, Brittany," of e-mailing have merged in some minds to form this greeting: "Dear Winnifred;"

A semicolon never follows a salutation. The use of commas or colons in greetings is a matter of formality or familiarity. It's your choice. You can either use a colon and make it a formal salutation or use a comma or dash and make it an informal salutation. Of course, it's up to you whether Brittany's your best friend, your beloved boss, or your bewitching colleague. The following greetings are arranged from very formal to very informal.

Dear Mr. Raymer:
Dear Mr. Raymer,
Dear Spike:
Dear Spike,

Spike,

Spike—(very informal, as in "picking up from the last conversation")

MEMORY TIP

Using a semicolon to punctuate a salutation is as inappropriate as eating with a toothbrush. It's the wrong tool.

51

She Needs No Introduction

COMMAS TO INTRODUCE

You've heard emcees introduce speakers with this line, "Here's a man who needs no introduction. . . ." Unlike that clichéd opening, some main thoughts in sentences do need an introductory word, phrase, or clause.

And when those introductory comments are not set off by a comma, they can cause misreading—as they do in the following passage:

> Be certain your paycheck is protected with disability income insurance. Only one in four workers has group or individual disability insurance to protect their incomes if they become disabled. Even those few who do have it through their employer, and there are limits to the amount of protection and how long the benefits are paid.

Did you do a double take on that last sentence? "Even those few who do have it through their employer" WHAT? What about even those few who do have it through their employer? I kept rereading and rereading, trying to figure out the meaning. Staring at the paragraph, I sat dumbfounded that such a nonsensical statement could have slipped through all the editors and proofreaders of this typically well-edited magazine.

Finally, the meaning surfaced. This was a case of a missing introductory comma, not an incomplete thought. (Insert a comma after *do*.)

> Be certain your paycheck is protected with disability income insurance. Only one in four workers has group or individual disability insurance to protect their incomes if they become disabled. Even those few who do *[have group or individual disability insurance]*, have it through their employer, and there are limits to the amount of protection and how long the benefits are paid.

Big difference. Generally speaking, use a comma after introductory words, phrases, or clauses to help readers quickly skim to the major idea of the sentence:

> Honestly, I am pleased with this product.
> Disappointed by the results on the job, he resigned.
> Before you leave, please explain the pricing options.
> Having heard the ad during the Super Bowl, they were prepared for the competitive reaction.
> In the first few months of the product launch, the salespeople seem more highly motivated to call on inactive accounts than they do later in the campaign.

MEMORY TIP

Although the pause should not be your general method of punctuation, it's a good rule of thumb for placing introductory commas. Consider yourself an actor: If you feel the need to pause after delivering the introductory word, phrase, or clause in your script, add the introductory comma.

52

Punctuation Powerless

Run-Ons—Semicolons Slip-Sliding Away

The antithesis of comma hiccups (tossing in commas for no good reason) is omitting necessary punctuation. The big punctuation pitfall in this category that renders a sentence powerless is the run-on. It's as noticeable as a train wreck.

Here are examples of sentence collisions:

Incorrect:

She loves her job however she's going to resign.

Ebeneezer outlined his goals for the new year, they seem very realistic and doable for the time frame.

Ziggy has asked for a reduced work schedule she wants to work no more than 30 hours a week.

Pongo has exceeded his budget, therefore, the remainder of his plans will need to be put on hold until next year.

Each of these sentences has two separate thoughts that can stand alone. Both "halves" of each sentence have a subject and a verb and can exist as a separate sentence. They have to be either written as two separate sentences or separated within the sentence by a semicolon. (When two separate thoughts are joined by connective adverbs like *however, therefore, thus, hence, moreover, consequently,* and *subsequently,* a comma doesn't have the strength to hold them apart.)

Correct:

She loves her job; however, she's going to resign. (Or: She loves her job. However, she's going to resign.)

Ebeneezer outlined his goals for the new year; they seem very realistic and doable for the time frame. (Or: Ebeneezer outlined his goals for the new year. They seem very realistic and doable for the time frame.)

Ziggy has asked for a reduced work schedule; she wants to work no more than 30 hours a week. (Or: Ziggy has asked for a reduced work schedule. She wants to work no more than 30 hours a week.)

Pongo has exceeded his budget; therefore, the remainder of his plans will need to be put on hold until next year. (Or: Pongo has exceeded his budget. The remainder of his plans will need to be put on hold until next year.)

Consider word flow in a document much like the traffic flow in our transportation system. A period means stop. A semicolon tells the reader to stop but to keep idling because there's another very closely related idea to follow. When writers fail to put punctuation signals in place appropriately, ideas crash in the reader's mind.

MEMORY TIP

Visualize this error as a train wreck. Two separate trains of thought crash into each other.

53

One Car, Two Cars, Three Cars, Four

COMMAS TO SEPARATE EQUAL THINGS

Have you ever sat at a railroad crossing and watched as car after car after car after car passes, with no end to the train in sight? Some people write and speak that way—an unending ramble, with no destination in sight.

Maybe you've heard an excited child tell a saga something like this: "I was outside playing and this big dog came up and started barking and we couldn't see what he was barking at so we started following him because he was running back and forth toward the sidewalk and the swings and then we noticed his leg was hurt and Tony tried to pat him but he pulled away and started barking even louder and then this guy came up and said the dog belonged to him and he started yelling at us to stop bothering his dog but we weren't doing anything to his dog except trying to see if his foot was hurt because it looked like it was bleeding."

You want to tell the child, "Just take a breath. Relax." This same sort of loosey-goosey writing sometimes creeps into engineering proposals, audit reports, and management e-mails. The writer drafts nine clauses without a comma or period to separate them.

Every time you write a complete thought (an independent clause—a group of words with a subject and a verb that stands alone), you have a choice of punctuation:

1. End with a period.
2. End with a semicolon followed by another closely related complete thought.
3. End with a comma and one of seven linking words, before joining another closely related complete thought.

If you select option 3, here are the seven linking words: *and, but, so, or, for, nor,* and *yet.* That's it. Those seven and no more. Not a tough list. *And, but,* or *so* will be appropriate about 90 percent of the time. The other four words will share the spotlight the remaining 10 percent of the time.

When joining independent items with one of those seven linking words, separate them with commas.

▶ Independent clauses joined by coordinate conjunctions (*and, but, or, so, nor, for, yet*)

▶ Items in a series ("Brunhilda brought water, crackers, and gum on the plane.")

▶ Distinct adjectives when they equally describe the noun or pronoun ("Pudge was a cantankerous, belligerent man.")

MEMORY TIP

Back to the traffic metaphor: Picture yourself sitting in your car at the entrance ramp to a major tollway. You've tossed your money into the collection basket. The green light flashes, and the gate arm lifts to permit one car to enter the flow of traffic. The gate arm separates each car as it enters the tollway.

The comma serves the same function between the flow of equal, independent items in a series or sentence.

54

The Alpha and the Omega

ENCLOSING COMMAS COME IN PAIRS

Ding-dong. Zigzag. Yin-yang. Just as some words need to serve in pairs to convey their full meaning, enclosing commas come in pairs.

These enclosing commas set off nonessential information from the rest of the sentence. As a traffic signal, they tell readers, "Slow down and look out the window here; see the additional intriguing scenes off the main path as we pass."

The common mistake with enclosing commas is that writers, like drivers, get in a hurry. They add the first comma of the pair and forget to add the final comma. (Maybe you have one of these people in your household: They open cabinet drawers and forget to shut them. They open packages and forget to discard the wrapping. They borrow things and forget to return them. They wear clothes and forget to put them in the laundry. Recognize a lifestyle here?)

Back to enclosing commas:

Incorrect:

Lancelot, my brother who lives in Ohio came to visit for the holidays.

▶ 153 ◀

Correct:

Lancelot, my brother who lives in Ohio, came to visit for the holidays.

Incorrect:

The client called Friday, March 21 about the contract.

Correct:

The client called Friday, March 21, about the contract.

Incorrect:

The clients asked about prices expecting them to be much higher than last year, but they were pleased to learn that we have not had an increase. (The first enclosing comma is missing.)

Correct:

The clients asked about prices, expecting them to be much higher than last year, but they were pleased to learn that we have not had an increase. (The second comma serves two purposes: it sets off the nonessential phrase and also joins the two independent clauses.)

Like parentheses, enclosing commas come in sets. Consider the word or group of words you're setting off from the rest of the sentence. Then add the commas on both ends of that group of words. (Of course, if the second comma of the enclosing pair falls at the end of a sentence, use a period instead.)

MEMORY TIP

Relate enclosing commas to bookends or parentheses. Use them as a set.

55

Colon Scope—Here's the Scoop

COLONS BEFORE A LIST

As a traffic signal, colons tell readers to come to a stop, keep idling, and look ahead. They stress, or highlight, what follows. They represent a bigger break than semicolons, but not quite a complete stop like periods.

They introduce either a series or a list that follows. That list may be either a formal list of items set up with bullets, dashes, or icons or an informal list of words and phrases to complete the sentence. Examples:

Please input the following information:
—Employee ID
—Department password
—Social security number
Please bring pertinent information to the meeting: travel expenses, trip reports, leads, and survey responses.
Bentley becomes bent out of shape about employees not performing at their best and shares his philosophy routinely: Fire them.

Here's the common mistake: putting a colon after a verb or an object of a preposition. Instead, the part before the colon must be able to stand alone as a complete thought.

Incorrect:

Please mail me: a travel pillow, steamer, suit, and shoes.

Correct:

Please mail me a travel pillow, steamer, suit, and shoes.

Please mail me these items: a travel pillow, steamer, suit, and shoes.

Incorrect:

Company officers include: Snuffy Smith, Bako Patel, and Amery Barrow.

Correct:

Company officers include Snuffy Smith, Bako Patel, and Amery Barrow.

Company officers include these individuals: Snuffy Smith, Bako Patel, and Amery Barrow.

Incorrect:

We are planning to open factories in: Kuala Lumpur, Bangkok, Sydney, and Caracas.

Correct:

We are planning to open factories in Kuala Lumpur, Bangkok, Sydney, and Caracas.

We are planning to open factories in these cities: Kuala Lumpur, Bangkok, Sydney, and Caracas.

Note one exception: A colon after the verb can be correct if used to set off a formal list. For example:

Our presentation covered several key points. They were:

▶ Talent management
▶ Structural management
▶ Relationship capital
▶ Rights allocation

Just as a car comes to a stop and honks its horn before it pulls into a parade, a clause, complete and full of air, must stop and honk before it starts into a list. The colon is that blaring horn: "Here comes a parade."

MEMORY TIP

The words before a colon must be able to stand alone as a complete sentence. If they don't, a colon is incorrect. (Exception: a colon before a formal list)

56

Fragmented Thoughts

UNINTENTIONAL FRAGMENTS

Don't do as I do; do as I say. This principle has never worked with my kids, so I doubt that it's going to go over well with you here without further explanation. Why? You'll find fragments (incomplete sentences) throughout this book. You'll also find them in the most technical engineering reports, Wall Street analysts' reports, and legal briefs.

Question: So why am I calling them a big mistake?

The operative word here is *intentional* fragments. In the previous paragraphs, *Why?* and *Question:* are not sentences. Neither has a subject or a verb. You can tell, however, that they're intentional expressions of complete thoughts, not careless errors.

You may have read e-mails from colleagues that contain fragments. Although they're often in a hurry. You see what I mean? That last thought, "although they're often in a hurry," appears to be an unintentional, incomplete thought written either because I was in a hurry or because some proofreader went to sleep on the job. You're thinking, "although they're often in a hurry" what?

Solution: double-check *although* and *because* clauses to make sure they're complete sentences. If you have other fragments (word groups with no subject and verb), make sure that they're intentional and that they express clear, complete thoughts. If they don't, turn them into sentences—usually by adding a missing verb.

If you have a particularly long group of words and you can't tell whether it's a sentence, try to add a tag question on the end. If that doesn't work, then you don't have a sentence. Example:

> When the auditors finish reviewing the security procedures this week, they will write and submit a formal report, *won't they?* (A tag question added to the end makes sense. This is a complete sentence.)
>
> When the auditors finish reviewing the security procedures this week, *aren't they? (don't they? can't they? haven't they?)* (A tag question added to the end makes no sense, so this is not a sentence.)

MEMORY TIP

Think classified ads: "Condo for Sale: 4 years old. Oceanside view. 3 miles from shopping. 2-car garage. $145K. Will consider lease." These brief, complete thoughts are intentional fragments. On the other hand, unintentional fragments convey fractured thinking.

57

Would You Send Me Your Address Please

INDIRECT QUESTIONS AND
SOFTENED COMMANDS

Picture yourself walking into your boss's office. He or she says to you, "So, . . . tell me what's on your mind." It sounds like a command, but from the smile and the body language, you take it as a true question and an invitation to talk—but only if you want to.

Same scene a week later: the boss says to you, "Can you send me a project update by this afternoon." The phrasing sounds like a question, but the frown and the tone let you know that it's actually a directive.

With such experience in the background, it's no wonder that we have trouble distinguishing a direct question from an indirect question and even a softened command. And that decision determines the proper punctuation. So here are the rules:

▶ Use a question mark with a direct question.

   Do you have enough staff to meet the deadline?
   He asked, "Do you have enough staff to meet the deadline?"

▶ Use a period with an indirect question.

Ebeneezer asked if I had enough staff to meet the deadline.

The client wondered whether Max could handle that high-pressure culture.

The president questioned Mesick about how he liked New Zealand.

▶ Use a period with a softened directive phrased as a question.

Would you send the report to me immediately at my office address.

Would you let me know if anyone deviates from this procedure.

Will someone please give me a call if you need more forms.

Will you please close my account, effective today.

Consider press conferences and how often reporters make political statements disguised as questions. Remember: A question is not a question until it's punctuated as such.

MEMORY TIP

Think scriptwriting. If you can "hear" someone asking the question, punctuate it as a question. If you're simply telling us about what question someone asked, don't. If your question is really a softened request or directive, use a period.

58

Can You Hear Me Now?

INDIRECT QUOTATIONS

You've heard them referred to as "he said/she said" situations, meaning that nobody can prove anything; it's just one person's word against the other's. You could label this situation with quotation marks the same way: If you don't use them correctly, the reader can't separate what was actually spoken from hearsay—that is, your own synthesis, interpretation, and conclusions about the other person's comments.

In short, quotation marks carry clout.

Incorrect:

> Trixy says that she "hates her job and plans to resign at the end of the year whether she has another job offer or not." (The writer here is only summarizing what Trixy said—and he may or may not have interpreted her comments correctly.)

Correct:

> Trixy said, "I hate my job. I'm resigning at the end of the year whether I have another job offer or not!" (These are Trixy's exact words.)

Here's what causes confusion: Occasionally, you want to quote just a word or phrase from the speaker, and you want to make sure that your reader knows that the original speaker used that exact phrasing—even if you've just summarized the rest of the comment. That's when you may add quotation marks around only a few words of the complete statement:

> Trixy's dissatisfaction here goes beyond boredom. She said that she actually "hated" her job.

Another example:

> Actually, our manager likes the "take-no-prisoners attitude on the trade floor" that he often mentions to the sales team; he thinks it intimidates our competitors during the convention.

Remember: If you're going to write someone's actual words, put them in quotation marks. If you're just going to summarize, don't.

MEMORY TIP

Quotation marks are for scriptwriters and the movies: If you can hear it, enclose it.

59

Inside or Outside?

WHERE, OH WHERE, DO THE QUOTATION MARKS GO?

You're going to want to argue with me on this one, so be forewarned. The common mistake is following logic in the placement of quotation marks when they fall next to other punctuation marks. The rules on this issue are illogical. So, let me give you the lowdown on how these rules evolved.

When periods, commas, colons, semicolons, and question marks fall next to quotation marks, you treat them differently—according to their size.

▶ Periods and commas always go INSIDE quotation marks—regardless of the meaning.

▶ Semicolons and colons always go OUTSIDE quotation marks—regardless of the meaning.

▶ Question marks and exclamation marks can go INSIDE or OUTSIDE quotation marks—DEPENDING on the meaning.

(Forgive me for shouting at you with the uppercase here, but that's because I don't want you to doze off and miss those important key words.)

So how did we get in this predicament? Back in the days before printing was automated, real people served as typesetters (no, not Bill Gates and Michael Dell). They actually placed wooden or metal letters into a case (the case looked like a jewelry box with many rows separated into compartments). Once the case was filled with all the letters to make a block of text, the printer turned the case over and imprinted the letters onto paper. (I know this may be hard to visualize, but bear with me here.)

There was no problem with the full-size letters staying in place when the case was turned upside down. But the smaller punctuation marks—namely, the commas and periods—frequently fell out of the case when the typesetter tipped it over to press it onto the paper.

So printers, being practical people, simply decided to move those little troubling commas and periods to the inside of the larger quotation marks. Those bigger marks helped hold the smaller marks in place. Over time, the printers overpowered the grammarians of the day. The rules for quotation marks changed forever.

So let me sum up by giving you some illogical but correctly punctuated sentences as examples.

Correct:
> He hates signing "contracts." (Yes, the period belongs to the whole sentence. But meaning doesn't matter. When a period falls next to a quotation mark, it goes inside.)
> He hates signing "contracts," but the vendor needs the paperwork. (Yes, the comma separates the two halves of the sentence. But meaning doesn't matter. When the comma falls next to a quotation mark, it goes inside.)

If the ad says "standard accommodations," be wary.

Pongo claims that standard accommodations are better than, "Sorry, but we have no more rooms available."

Dilbert dislikes auditors trained in "best practices"; those "best practices" always seem to be working in organizations unlike ours. (This semicolon looks correct—and it is. It separates two halves of the sentence.)

The contract specifies "light snacks": fruit, cheeses, and crackers. (This colon looks correct—and it is. It follows the complete first half of the sentence and precedes the list.)

Our executives may have been watching too much TV when they came up with this year's theme of "Executing with the Stars": we even vote people off the payroll. (This colon looks correct—and it is. It follows the complete first half of the sentence and highlights the second half of the sentence.)

The brochure raises this question: "Why go elsewhere for the best meal in town?" (The question mark is fickle; its placement depends on meaning. This sentence is correct because only the part inside the quotation marks is the question.)

The ER nurse continued to ask the elderly patient, "Are you in pain?" (Only the part inside the quotation marks is a question, so the question mark belongs inside as well.)

Is real estate investing still primarily about "location, location, location"? (The question mark goes outside the quotation marks because the entire sentence is the question, not just the part inside the quotation marks.)

One exception: For all of you who learned British English, you can go on your merry way and forget this nonsense. In the British system of punctuation, quotation marks are placed logically—periods, commas, question marks, and so forth can go inside or outside the quotation marks, depending on the meaning of the sentence.

Also, as a side note here, never use double punctuation. When two punctuation marks fall at the same place, use the stronger mark.

Incorrect:

> Spike yelled, "I have the winning ticket!," but the emcee did not hear him.

Correct:

> Spike yelled, "I have the winning ticket!" but the emcee did not hear him.

MEMORY TIP

Think of that poor printer setting type by hand.

60

Ripley's Believe It or Not

QUOTATION MARKS TO CHANGE THE TONE OR THE MEANING

Quotation marks can imply sarcasm and tongue-in-cheek comments, so make sure that's what you intend when you use them. For example: "Spike flew to Los Angeles last week with his blonde 'associate' to tie up loose ends on a business deal before attending a trade show in the area." The use of quotation marks here tells me that the writer has his doubts that Spike and his associate will have their minds totally attuned to business deals.

A careless or loose use of quotation marks can reverse the meaning of a word or phrase.

The same holds true when tossing a lighthearted word or phrase into a formal document or vice versa:

Except to the extent that you state otherwise, this document gives the person you name as your agent the authority to make any and all health-care decisions for you in accordance with your wishes, including your religious and moral beliefs, when you are no longer capable of making them yourself. If you do not have a physician, you should talk with someone who is knowledgeable about these issues before signing—not necessarily "*your Uncle Fred*," but someone who can provide legal assistance on these matters.

So to sum up: Use quotation marks to enclose misnomers, coined words, slang terms, or tongue-in-cheek comments that don't match the tone or style of the rest of the document.

MEMORY TIP

Consider some quotation marks as winks. They change the meaning or tone of the actual words.

61

Spare Tires

SINGLE QUOTATION MARKS

Think of single quotation marks as you would spare tires for your car. You don't routinely drive your car on a spare tire. Typically, your spare tire is of lower quality than the regular set. You use it only in case of emergency, like a blowout. As soon as you get to a service station, you get the blowout repaired and return the spare to your trunk.

That's the idea behind the use of single quotation marks. They're used only in emergencies—when the sentence or passage already has quotation marks around it.

Incorrect:

Beulah has 'fine-tuned' her approach to performance appraisals.
Hortense told the committee: 'My job is secure.'

Correct:

Beulah has "fine-tuned" her approach to performance appraisals.
Hortense told the committee: "My job is secure."

Single quotation marks are correct only when they are used inside double quotation marks.

Correct:

Their key manager provided us very little detail in responding to the client's Request for Proposal #45621. The client's e-mail stated only, "Your bid 'whether submitted by e-mail, uploaded to our Web site, or faxed' must include all assigned consultants, along with a list of their advanced degrees." (The part in single quotations is being quoted exactly from the Request for Proposal document.)

I told my staff this morning, "Ebeneezer e-mailed me that he had become a 'glorified beach bum' since his retirement."

According to the *Wall Street Journal*, attorneys "are confused and angry over this Supreme Court ruling and fear 'catastrophic change' is another scare tactic of terrorist groups working behind the scenes to control our court systems."

MEMORY TIP

Use single quotation marks as you would spare tires—when the double marks are unavailable (already in use).

PART 7

Perplexing Possessives

No, we are not talking about demonic possession—or even possessive mothers-in-law or spouses. Here's the concept: Make words singular or plural, and then show ownership by adding either an apostrophe or an apostrophe and an –s. If the word already ends in an –s, don't add another –s unless you pronounce the extra –s as a separate syllable.

Examples: "Ebeneezer drove *Chris's* car to the company party and had a great time. But on the way home, things happened. He lost the *Joneses'* house keys, hit a *cop's* car, and crashed into his *boss's* front gate. He was just lucky that the *children's* bedroom was not located at the front of the house and that they were unharmed. And that was just the beginning of his trouble. An eyewitness to both his mishaps called the police, who showed up immediately to ticket him. As they searched his car, the police officers discovered that both *bosses'* laptops with the *company's* trade secrets had been stolen from the trunk of his car. Officer James *Potts's* investigative report contained comments from the eyewitness that Ebeneezer appeared to be talking on a cell phone and watching a DVD while the car was in motion."

Chris's car (singular; then add apostrophe and –s to show possession)

the Joneses' house keys (plural; then show possession with the apostrophe; the plural form ends in –s already, so no extra –s is

added to show possession because the extra syllable is not pronounced)

cop's car (singular; then add apostrophe and –*s* to show possession)

boss's front gate (singular; then add apostrophe and –*s* to show possession)

children's bedroom (plural; then add apostrophe and –*s* to show possession)

bosses' laptops (plural; then add apostrophe to show possession; the
word ends in –*s* already, so no extra –*s* to show possession
because the extra syllable is not pronounced)

company's trade secrets (singular; then add apostrophe and –*s* to
show possession)

James Potts's (singular; then add apostrophe and –*s* to show possession)

Visualize the apostrophe as the line of demarcation—the dividing
line, the line that says end of the singular or plural word, the point that
says, *stop*. What comes at the point of the apostrophe adds another
twist to the word altogether—the idea of ownership.

The chapters in this section detail the most common mistakes with
possessives.

62

Whatever Possessed Me!

IT'S VERSUS *ITS*

People sometimes cement in their minds that apostrophes show ownership and jump to this conclusion: *It's* shows ownership. That's logical thinking, but the wrong conclusion.

Apostrophes show ownership with *nouns*: Jake's desk, Ziggy's job, Jamale's commission check. But *pronouns* already have possessive forms without apostrophes: *his, her, hers, your, yours, my, mine, our, ours, their, theirs, whose, its.*

Tossing an apostrophe into any of these pronouns is incorrect.

Incorrect:

their's, ours', your's, hers', his'

Another use altogether for an apostrophe is to show missing letters, such as in a contraction: *don't, can't, I'll, they've.* Like these other contractions, the word *it's* is a contraction, meaning *it is.*

Incorrect:

The building was damaged; it's roof was leaking after the rain.

Correct:

The building was damaged; its roof was leaking after the rain.

When you're confused between the two choices, substitute *it is*. If that's your meaning, you need the words that can be broken into two parts. Example: "It's tires are damaged." Substitute and read, "It is tires are damaged," and you'll know that you have the wrong word. Example: "It's too late to help." Substitute and read, "It is too late to help," and you'll know that you have the correct word.

If the substitution doesn't work, you're showing ownership and need no apostrophe—just like *his*, *hers*, *theirs*, *yours*, and *ours*.

MEMORY TIP

Substitute *it is* in the sentence. If the substitution works, use *it's*.

63

Who's on First?

WHOSE VERSUS WHO'S

Closely related to the issue with *it's* and *its* is the matter of *whose* and *who's*. Same song, second verse. These pronouns are already possessives without apostrophes: *his, her, hers, your, yours, my, mine, our, ours, their, theirs, whose,* and *its.* Adding an apostrophe in any of these pronouns is overkill, over the top, incorrect. So stop it.

The pronoun *whose* shows ownership: "Whose workbook is lying in the training room?" *Who's,* on the other hand, is a contraction of *who is.*

Incorrect:

Who's building is located across the freeway?

Correct:

Whose building is located across the freeway?

Incorrect:

Whose going to the seminar on Friday?

Correct:

Who's (who is) going to the seminar on Friday?

MEMORY TIP

Substitute *who is* in the sentence. If the substitution works, use *who's*.

64

Why Are You So Possessive?

PLURALS CONFUSED WITH POSSESSIVES

Just like the Lay's commercial says about aficionados who can't eat just one potato chip, some people start playing with apostrophes and can't use just one. They toss them in everywhere to make words plurals.

Plural means more than one. To say we're a pluralistic society means that we have many interests, stemming from different backgrounds. Possession (shown with apostrophes), on the other hand, indicates ownership. Possession has nothing to do with plurals. And plurals have nothing particularly to do with ownership.

Although these are two separate concepts, using a possessive form instead of the simple plural noun is a common mistake. Don't add an apostrophe when you only need to show that there's more than one of something or somebody.

Incorrect:

We have six supplier's involved in this project.

Employee's frequently forget their badges.

Company officials' do not approve of these practices.

The trial balances and reconciliations' have been sent to the controller for review.

The inspectors sent reports detailing all the deficiencies' and recommendations.

Correct:

We have six suppliers involved in this project

Employees frequently forget their badges.

Company officials do not approve of these practices.

The trial balances and reconciliations have been sent to the controller for review.

The inspectors sent reports detailing all the deficiencies and recommendations.

One exception: apostrophes can be used to show plurals of letters and numerals:

She earned four A's this semester. (Without the apostrophe, the As might be mistaken for the word *as*.)

In case we have further lock-ups, Pongo ordered several 267CV's as spare parts for the system. (Without the apostrophe here, the –s might be understood as part of the serial number.)

Not all parents are possessive, and not all plurals are possessive. Only plurals that own something need apostrophes.

MEMORY TIP

Plurals and possessives have nothing in common but the letter *p*.

65

Yours, Mine, and Ours

JOINT OWNERSHIP—WHO GETS THE APOSTROPHE?

Is it Percival and Winnifred's home or Percival's and Winnifred's home? Is it Depak and Daffy's tenure on the board of directors or Depak's and Daffy's tenure? When you have multiple owners, who gets the apostrophe? Well, that depends.

If the two people own something jointly, show ownership only on the last name. But if they own something separately, show ownership on both names:

Percival and Winnifred's home (they share the same home)
Percival's and Winnifred's homes (they each have a home)
Depak and Daffy's tenure (they served together on the board)
Depak's and Daffy's tenure (they did not necessarily serve at the same time)

Remember, too, that you can also show ownership by flipping the phrase and using the word *of*: "This is the home of Percival and Winnifred."

When the two owners are pronouns, place the noun between them: Not "*Your* or *my* house?" But "*My* house or *yours*?" Even if only one owner is a pronoun, it sounds better to place the noun between them: "I reviewed Horatio's e-mails and yours before the meeting."

As a side note, *I* can never be possessive. (I'm not speaking personally, of course.) Here's a common error in casual conversation:

Incorrect:

Horatio and I's suggestion would save the company almost $2 million.

Correct:

Horatio's suggestion and mine would save the company almost $2 million.

▼

MEMORY TIP

If two people share ownership, they also have to share the apostrophe.

66

Do You Love *Me*—Or What I Can *Do* for You?

POSSESSIVES BEFORE GERUNDS

What do these sentences have in common?

"Do you mind me smoking?"
"Our city ordinance restricts him driving while talking on a cell phone."
"I heard him sneezing."

All three of them are wrong. They should be correctly written this way:

"Do you mind *my* smoking?"
"Our city ordinance restricts *his* driving while talking on a cell phone."
"I heard *his* sneezing."

Here's why: the *–ing* word or phrase (verb plus *–ing*) that follows is playing the role of a noun (person, place, thing, or idea), not a descriptive word. (The grammatical term for this construction is a gerund: a verb ending in *–ing* serving as a noun.)

If you substitute another noun for the *–ing* words in the previous sentences, you'll see the point quickly.

"Do you mind *me accent?*" (strange, eh?)
"Do you mind *my accent?*" (easy to understand with a plain noun)

"Our city ordinance restricts *him gun.*" (strange, eh?)
"Our city ordinance restricts *his gun.*" (easy to understand with a
    plain noun)

"I heard *him outburst.*" (strange, eh?)
"I heard *his outburst.*" (easy to understand with a plain noun)

Here's what complicates things: Sometimes both versions of a sentence (with and without the possessive form) can be correct because both are logical meanings. Here's an example where that's true:

The boss resents that engineer's highlighting his mistakes in the
    meeting.
The boss resents that engineer highlighting his mistakes in the
    meeting.

In the first example, the boss resents what the engineer did in the meeting. In the second example, the boss resents the engineer himself. The fact that he was highlighting his mistakes in the meeting simply identifies which engineer the boss is talking about among several engineers who may work there.

My point: the correct form of the pronoun dictates the meaning of the sentence.

Memory Tip

Ask this simple question: are you emphasizing the person or the person's action? If your point is the action, use the possessive form before the activity.

67

It's About Time

POSSESSIVES WITH TIME AND AMOUNTS

In cover letters accompanying résumés and biographies in sales proposals, phrases like these run rampant. Can you identify the common mistake in each?

Incorrect:

Have ten years experience in . . .

Worked at Universal, where I led the sales team to sell $40 million worth of product X . . .

Was awarded the Most Valuable Team Member for the outstanding third-quarter production of the wing design . . .

In English, we make certain expressions of time and money possessive. So such phrases need either an apostrophe or the word *of* to show that "ownership."

Correct:

Have ten years' experience in . . .

Worked at Universal, where I led the sales team to sell $40 million of product X . . .

Daffy was awarded the Most Valuable Team Member for the outstanding third-quarter's production of the wing design . . .

MEMORY TIP

People are possessive of their time, money, and experience. Use apostrophes to express ownership or duration of time in that same sense.

68

Overly Possessive

DESCRIPTIVE OR POSSESSIVE?

Should you use the possessive form in situations like the following?

"I have a copy of Universal's contract."
Or: "I have a copy of the Universal contract."

"Should we interrupt the attorneys' meeting?"
Or: "Should we interrupt the attorneys meeting?"

Actually, you can't go wrong here. Either is correct—but with due diligence. And I don't mean to get caught in a legal loop with you here.

Let's take on the lawyers first. The possessive form (with the apostrophe) means that the meeting belongs to the attorneys. They arranged it; they control it; it's their song and dance to do with as they please (if lawyers ever sing and dance).

Without the apostrophe, this is a meeting of attorneys. For all we know, prison officials or Congress may have forced these attorneys to show up. The word *attorneys* is simply a descriptive term, as in *school board meeting* or *pharmaceutical meeting*.

Now, about the Universal contract: the possessive form (with the apostrophe) means that Universal owns the contract—Universal originated the contract terms and the offer. Without the apostrophe, *Universal* simply describes the contract. The writer is referring to the Universal contract, not the Wal-Mart contract or the Exxon contract. The contract may be one that the writer is preparing to force Universal to sign, sight unseen.

Apostrophes may be small marks, but they carry big meaning.

MEMORY TIP

Is the noun descriptive or possessive? If somebody owns or controls something, use the possessive form. If the word merely describes something, don't.

PART 8

Reminders About Redundancies

My most valuable learning experience in graduate school happened to be my most humiliating. Having read the first hundred pages of my master's thesis, one of my thesis directors, a literary prize–winning novelist himself, handed back my novel with downcast eyes and mumbled something about "needs to be tightened."

One line of his scathing review of my first draft came through distinctly: "Here's a good page."

"One good page?" I'd written what I considered more than 100 good pages.

He pulled page 67 from the stack—a lively scene of dialogue on which he'd scrawled "Excellent" across the top.

I stared at it for quite some time to determine what magic had been at play there, but missing elsewhere. I agreed that it looked brilliant— but no different from the other 99 pages he'd effectively relegated to the shredder.

"Would you edit a page to show me what's so . . . redundant in the rest?"

Sullenly and without a word, he picked up a red pen and began to slash through words, phrases, and sentences as if they were road kill. Horrified as his pen obliterated metaphor after simile after prepositional phrase, I sat stunned when he handed me the edited page, about one-fourth its original length.

That process gave me both pain and pleasure. Watching him chop, splice, and shape significance out of the simple proved to be the most valuable 15 minutes of my writing career. Redundancy has been a dirty word ever since.

Everyone in the business world, it seems, understands the value of "getting to the point." The problem? Identifying what to leave out and what to include. The good news? Most of the time, you don't have to sacrifice information to be brief. Redundancy involves using unnecessary words to express the same idea. That's the subject of this section— helping you root out the rot.

69

Past Experience—Is There Any Other Kind?

LITTLE-WORD PADDING AND REDUNDANT IDEAS

Ideas have tremendous power if undiluted with superfluous words. Although the following clichés seep from the most seasoned writers on occasion, they clutter a speech, a conversation, or a document. Stamp them out so that your ideas stand out. The wordy phrases in the following chart can often be replaced by the word inside the parentheses.

Padding With No Purpose	
in the amount of (for)	on account of the fact that (since, because)
for the purpose of (for)	for the reason that (since, because)
in reference to (about)	to say nothing of (and)
with reference to (about)	in view of the foregoing circumstances (because)
in connection with (about)	it is therefore apparent that (so)

with regard to (about)	along the lines of (like, as)
pertaining to (about)	in the nature of (like)
to be in a position to (to)	by means of (by)
in order to (to)	until such time as you (when)
in order that (to)	with the exception of (except)
with a view toward (to)	the question as to whether (whether)
for the express purpose of (to)	in conjunction with (with)
in the event that (if)	if at all possible (if possible)
if it should turn out that (if)	in all other cases (otherwise)
if and when (if)	a sufficient number of (enough)
unless and until (unless)	in the vicinity of (near)
if it is assumed that (if)	it would seem that (it seems)
inasmuch as (as)	it would thus appear that (apparently, probably)
in spite of the fact that (although)	it may well be that (perhaps, maybe)
with the result that (so)	in a satisfactory manner (satisfactorily)
by the same token (similarly)	after this has been done (then)
on a regular basis (regularly)	at this precise moment in time (now)

in most cases (usually)	at the present time (now)
in all cases (always, all)	at this point in time (now)
at all times (always)	at this time (now)
not infrequently (often)	at an early date (soon)
numerous times (often, frequently)	at a later date (later)
until such time as (until, when)	whether or not (whether)
during the time that (while)	of a confidential nature (confidentially)
a large number of (many)	may or may not (may)
on two separate occasions (twice)	in the very near future (soon)

Redundant Ideas

alternative choices	conclusive proof
desirable benefits	true facts
basic fundamentals	honest truth
important essentials	consensus of opinion
basic essentials	final completion
main essentials	advance warning
serious crisis	adequate enough
necessary requisite	disappear from sight

close together	following after
end result	equally as effective as
current status	foreign imports
few and far between	any and all
final outcome	as a general rule
future plans	in actual fact
free gift	equally as well
past history	in two equal halves
early beginnings	symptoms indicative of
new breakthrough	completely surrounded
separate entities	as you may or may not know
different varieties	on pages 20–30 inclusive
empty space	this particular instance
close proximity	regular weekly meetings
surrounding circumstances	exactly alike
joint partnership	precisely correct
group meeting	

Repetition of a key idea occasionally serves a purpose—to emphasize an idea or to bridge from one point to another. But *needless* redundancy can ruin otherwise brilliant thinking.

MEMORY TIP

Think of little-word padding as layers of onion skin before you get to the usable part. Peel them from your writing.

70

Continue On

REDUNDANT VERB ADD-ONS

Another rung in the redundancy rundown involves tagging an unnecessary word onto a verb—a word whose meaning has already been captured in the verb itself. For example, consider the common phrase "continue on." *Continue* itself means "to go on" or "to move ahead." So to say "continue on" states the last word twice: "go on on."

Another example: "Ebeneezer is going to follow *up on* these stocks for the next month to see how they do." Why not just "follow these stocks"?

Take a look at the following list for a few other such verb add-ons.

Verb Add-Ons	
continue on	open up
refer back to	cancel out
consolidated together	delete out
grouped together	circulate around
joined together	first began

connect together	distribute out
combined together	send out
attach together	continue to remain
add together	still remain
link together	still continue
add up	still persist
try out	start out
plan ahead	balance against each other
repeat again	follow on
finish up	follow up

MEMORY TIP

Visualize a collapsible drinking cup for travelers. The meaning of the second word has already been collapsed into (incorporated in) the prior word.

71

A Subject Matter Worth Discussing

REDUNDANT NOUNS

Another redundant layer of onion skin involves pairing two nouns or a noun and an adjective to convey the same idea. We can discuss either the *subject* or the *matter*—your preference. But it would be the same two cents' worth.

Another example: "Our executive will visit the factories in the summer months." Why don't they just visit "in the summer"? Is it possible to visit in the summer years?

Redundancies: Paired Nouns, Adjectives, and Verbs Expressing the Same Idea	
subject matter	facts and figures
goals and objectives	cost the sum of $389
in this day and age	during the month of August
period of time	during the years 2009–2029 inclusive

point in time	winter months
orange in color	first and foremost
small in size	chief and primary
cylindrical in shape	valuable and important
a distance of 5,000 miles	separate and distinct
the time of day	separate and apart
1,500 words in length	ways and means
few in number	comings and goings
cease and desist	worry and concern
null and void	defend and protect

MEMORY TIP

If the phrase seems to roll off your tongue, consider that a clue. Stop and chop.

72

"The Reason Is Because . . . "

DOUBLESPEAK

This common redundancy merits its own chapter. A reason *is* a because. A reason *is* a why. To state, "The reason is because . . ." is like saying, "the report is the report," "the storm is the storm," "the decision was the decision."

Simply state the reason and move on:

The reason for his resignation was more money.
The reason she moved to Michigan was to be near her family.

MEMORY TIP

When you start to say, "the reason is because," ask yourself if you're stalling for an excuse.

73

Going to Bat for *Thats*

DO YOU NEED THE *THAT*?

Evidently some people go through life plopping *thats* into passages wherever possible to introduce a clause (group of words with a subject and verb):

> In the last three decades, we have discovered the extraordinary power of the brain *that* is incomprehensible to most of us. By staying focused through reinforcement in our desire to achieve this prize *that* has become the object of our promise, we enlist our mind to help us accomplish our objective. Remember earlier *that* we discussed *that* the primary function of the subconscious mind is self-preservation. This desire to protect us sometimes puts the subconscious mind in the role of an overprotective mother attempting to keep us from engaging in an activity *that* might cause us harm, pain, or embarrassment.

Other people go through life extracting *thats* from the same passages whenever possible:

> In the last three decades, we have discovered the extraordinary power of the brain incomprehensible to most of us. By staying focused through reinforcement in our desire to achieve this

prize *that* has become the object of our promise, we enlist our mind to help us accomplish our objective. Earlier we discussed *that* the primary function of the subconscious mind is self-preservation. This desire to protect us sometimes puts the subconscious mind in the role of an overprotective mother attempting to keep us from engaging in a harmful, painful, or embarrassing activity.

Usually this process of adding and deleting *thats* takes place on the same document between two colleagues who irritate each other. Notice that in the rewrite, only two of the five *thats* remain necessary for clarity. The last sentence also involves a slight rewording.

So when do you need a *that*? Let clarity be your guide:

Incorrect:

> The consultant warned us Thursday sales leads might drop. (Did the consultant warn them on Thursday? Or was the consultant's warning about Thursday sales leads?)

Correct:

> The consultant warned us that Thursday sales leads might drop.
> The consultant warned us Thursday that sales leads might drop.

Conclusion: You have choices about *that*. If clarity isn't an issue, *that* clutters. If you need *that* for clarity, by all means, use it.

(Note: For a discussion on *that* versus *which*, see Chapter 28, "Which Hunts," and for punctuation with *that* and *which*, see Chapter 48, "Comma Clauses and Pauses.")

MEMORY TIP

Dr. Seuss joined clauses with *that* when necessary to see how far his readers could go with the beat and one breath.

But Dr. Seuss made megamillions off his rhymes and his funny hats—not necessarily his *thats*.

74

I Get Your Point—But Do You Get Mine?

ET CETERA AND SO FORTH

Tossing out an *et cetera* is not the same as flashing someone a Wal-Mart gift card. With a gift card in hand, you can buy anything in the store—lettuce, lipstick, or luggage. *Et cetera*, on the other hand, means "in the same pattern, class, or category" or "in like manner."

Incorrect:

> When you attend the trade show, be sure to come prepared with everything you might need: brochures, surveys, vacuum, etc.

What's the clear pattern in the last sentence? Would you think to bring tennis shoes? How about paper clips? Drapery? A hole punch? An easel? A paintbrush? Bubble wrap? Only if you've worked a trade show booth previously when Murphy showed up and everything went wrong!

Correct:

> Please group these mock-ups into layouts of five items for the catalog; the even-numbered items 2, 4, 6, 8, and 10 will go on a single page, et cetera.

It's as if some people want to make sure you think hard about what goes in the sentence blank. They play pile-on: "If the new Realtor takes you to court, the lawyers are going to ask you about when you sold the land, how much you paid for it, why hadn't you looked for a buyer earlier, et cetera, et cetera, and so forth."

If you want other people to do the thinking for you, that's okay with me. Just give them a clear signal with "and so forth" or the slang "yada-yada." Those phrases say, "You fill in the blank with anything that comes to mind, and I'm happy." In any case, you don't need to pile on. One *et cetera, and so forth*, or *yada-yada* will do the trick.

▼

Memory Tip

Et cetera is like a discount coupon on a certain product the manufacturer wants you to buy: "$50 off any Sony TV from Best Buy before December 31." The manufacturer establishes a specific deal; you either participate or you don't—but you can't create your own details.

And so forth lets you cut your own deal.

75

"Where's He At?"

UNNECESSARY PREPOSITIONS

I can't help but think you've heard this one before. Oops—did it myself. Did you hear that just roll off my tongue? In the phrase *help but*, the *but* does nothing but butt in: "I can't help thinking you've heard this one before" captures the thought quite nicely, thank you.

Omit prepositions that have nothing to add to the meaning of the sentence:

Where did the e-mail go (to)?

The crate fell off (of) the truck during our move.

My boss wandered outside (of) the trade show lobby just before the client stopped by our booth.

That cafeteria is located opposite (of) my office.

Where's Ebeneezer (at) in terms of his sales career?

MEMORY TIP

When tempted to add an unnecessary preposition, remember this quip you may have heard long ago from a parent or teacher:

Sammy: "Where's my coat at?"

Parent: "Between the A and the T?"

The punch line? The preposition is unnecessary—so between the letters is a good place for something or someone to hide.

PART 9

Miscellaneous Matters

You've mastered all the major matters at this point. In this section, you'll see a hodgepodge of pet peeves that irritate your peers, your customers, and Uncle Pete. In the big scheme of things, these errors may not be all that's standing between us and world peace. But of the less-important concerns, these mistakes can cost you a contract, cut you from the global competition, or mar an otherwise stellar impression.

76

Oh, Say, Can You See?

MISPRONUNCIATION

Comedian Norm Crosby made a living with malapropisms. The term *malapropism* refers to the mistake of using a different word from the one the speaker or writer intends. The term is actually derived from Richard Sheridan's 1775 play *The Rivals*, in which the character Mrs. Malaprop frequently misspeaks, to great comic effect.

Here's an example: "What are you incinerating?" meaning "What are you insinuating?" Here's another recent one from *American Idol*: "I made a carnal sin; I forgot the words," meaning "cardinal sin." Another: "My manager is a vast suppository of information," meaning "My manager is a vast repository of information."

Malapropisms are not the mistake under discussion here. But mispronunciations can be equally embarrassing. Unless you intend to make comedy your day job, these can stall your career.

Certain common words have syllables that people routinely transpose. And once learned incorrectly, these words become dragons to slay. Here's a starter list. Because even your best friend won't tell you, check these out for yourself to create awareness.

> *relevant* (*re-le-vant*, often mispronounced *re-ve-lant*)
> *remuneration* (*re-mu-ner-a-tion*, often mispronounced *re-nu-mer-a-tion*)

nuclear (*nu-cle-ar*, often mispronounced *noo-cu-lar* as in particular)

candidate (*can-di-date*, often mispronounced *can-ni-date*)

escape (*es-cape*, often mispronounced *ex-cape*)

jewelry (*jew-el-ry*, often mispronounced *jew-le-ry*)

supposedly (*sup-pos-ed-ly*, often mispronounced *sup-pos-a-bly*)

asterisk (*as-ter-risk*, often mispronounced *as-te-rix* or *as-ter-icks*)

mispronunciation (*mis-pro-nun-ci-a-tion*, often mispronounced *mis-pro-noun-ci-a-tion*)

February (*Feb-roo-air-y*, often mispronounced *Feb-yoo-air-y*)

plenitude (*plen-i-tude*, often mispronounced *plent-i-tude*)

across (*a-cross*, often mispronounced *a-crost*)

MEMORY TIP

Visualize each word spread apart with its syllables separated until the correct pronunciation becomes second nature.

77

What Are the Odds to Start?

STARTING A SENTENCE WITH A NUMBER

Numerals and words should stand apart, like oil and water. But when a sentence begins with a numeral, that's not always the case.

Consider this confusing example: "The client sent the invoices showing the total amount. 6 percent had been altered in some aspect." The period from the previous sentence can be mistaken for a decimal in the numeral of the next sentence. (Is it 6 percent or .6 percent of the invoices that have been altered?)

To avoid this confusion, recast the sentence so that any numeral comes later in the sentence or so that a written number begins the sentence.

Incorrect:

$45 is due on our invoice.

Correct:

Our invoice shows $45 due.

Incorrect:

320 employees participated in the survey.

Correct:

We have had 320 employees participate in the survey.
The survey included 320 employee responses.

Correct but Looks Odd:

Forty-six percent voted last year; only 36 percent voted this year.

Better:

Last year, 46 percent voted; this year, only 36 percent voted.

MEMORY TIP

Don't start sentences with numbers. Why not? Decimals and periods are indistinguishable dots.

78

Nonsense

NONWORDS, FILLERS, AND COLLOQUIALISMS

Experts who count such things estimate that there are 470,000 words in the English language. So it's not as if we don't have enough legitimate words to choose from. But some of us seem to have nothing better to do with our time than wander around digging up additional words to toss into the cacophony:

Rufus, *like*, is laughing at lunch, *right*, and returns to his office. So I wait until he finishes, *okay*? And then I tell him that his department is being downsized and that we'll *orientate* all of them to finding a new job. They *ain't cuttin'* it. You know what I mean? That could be said of a *lot* of departments around here. *Follow me*? Then Rufus stops *cold* and *goes*, "*Alright. No problem.* I'm *fixing to* quit anyway." Even though he's *dark-complected*, I could tell by his face that he was upset. But he was trying hard to be *way cool* about it. But *irregardless* of what he said *and all*, *pretty much* anybody *could have told* that he was *bummed out* about it. I told the rest of *his people* in the department not to put callers who were trying to get *ahold* of him *thru* to him for the remainder of the day. I do agree, however, that people need to be *incentivized* better around here—both *salary-wise* and *morale-wise*. But you *gotta* do what you *gotta* do.

Do we use slang and colloquialisms when we talk? Sure. But there's a difference between slang and colloquialisms (appropriate for casual conversation on occasion) and nonwords and fillers (inappropriate).

Granted, sometimes new ideas do call for new words. But non-words describe ideas in odd ways.

MEMORY TIP

Check the dictionary before deciding to coin a new word. You're known by the company you keep and the words you speak.

79

"You Should of Known Better!"

CONTRACTIONS THAT AREN'T

Keynoters preach the pitfalls of *shoulda, coulda, woulda* negative self-talk. Their clever alliteration makes a great motivational speech, but it further garbles grammar for the strugglers. This common mistake results from letting the ear override the eye. That is, in the contractions *should've, would've,* and *could've,* the abbreviated *have* sounds like the preposition *of.* People become confused and actually write or say *should of, would of,* and *could of.*

A contraction is two words that have been contracted (or pulled) into one word: *they'd, there's, can't, we're, I'll, he's, they've, we'll, haven't.* These are proper contractions, acceptable in formal documents.

Others given here are slang, inappropriate for formal business communication.

The "of" Gang:

> *Could've, should've, might've, must've, would've.* I noted at the beginning of this chapter the way "the *of* gang" leads many people actually to write these words in formal documents as

could of, should of, and *would of* rather than *could have, should have,* and *would have.*

Random Contractions With Will:

That'll, this'll, it'll, what'll, there'll, where'll, there'll (that will, this will, it will, what will, there will, where will, there will)

Random Contractions With Would:

That'd, this'd, how'd, where'd, why'd, there'd, what'd, it'd (that would, this would, how would, where would, why would, there would, what would, it would)

Random Contractions With Is:

How's, when's, why's, where's (how is, when is, why is, where is)

Random Contractions With Are:

There're, when're, where're, why're, that're (there are, when are, where are, why are, that are)

Many of these contractions are part of our casual conversations because we take shortcuts when we talk. Guilty. But for formal writing, don't dare. As for the contractions in the following table, use them with my compliments. You're welcome.

Acceptable for Writing
I've (I have)
I'll (I will)
I'm (I am)

I'd (I would)

you've (you have)

you'll (you will)

you're (you are)

you'd (you would)

he's/she's (he or she is or he or she has)

he'll/she'll (he or she will)

he'd/she'd (he or she would)

they've (they have)

they'll (they will)

they're (they are)

they'd (they would or they had)

we've (we have)

we'll (we will)

we're (we are)

we'd (we would or we had)

let's (let us)

hadn't, haven't, hasn't (had not, have not, has not)

can't, couldn't (cannot, could not)

shouldn't (should not)

weren't, won't, wouldn't (were not, will not, would not)

don't, doesn't, didn't (do not, does not, did not)

oughtn't, mustn't, mightn't (ought not, must not, might not)

what're, what's (what are, what is or what has)

there's (there is)

MEMORY TIP

Beware of "contraction contortions." Visualize circus contortionists who twist themselves like human pretzels into all sorts of unnatural positions. *Legitimate* contractions typically have only one or two letters omitted; they look and sound natural. Words contracted into *unnatural* contortions are much less recognizable.

80

Got Trouble?

HAVE VERSUS GOT

Do you *have* trouble, or have you *got* trouble?

Replace *got* with *have* or *has* in situations when you mean having in possession. If you mean *gotten* in the sense that someone has received or acquired something, then by all means, grab it and go with it. Examples:

Clumsy:

Dilbert has got four engineers on his redesign team. (in possession)

Improved:

Dilbert has four engineers on his redesign team.

Clumsy:

Ebeneezer has got money to spend for his vacation. (in possession)

Improved:

Ebeneezer has money to spend for his vacation.

Clumsy:

Hortense has got a big decision to make this week.

Improved:

Hortense has a big decision to make this week.

Correct:

The company has gotten plenty of recognition for this award. (acquired, received)

I've gotten four complaints this month. (emphasis on received)

Also correct:

I have received four complaints this month.

MEMORY TIP

Think of baseball: the center fielder sees a fly ball coming toward him and yells, "I've *got* it!" as he lunges to make the catch. (He's acquiring the ball.) Once it's in his glove, he *has* it.

81

Make a Dash for It

DISTINCT USES FOR HYPHENS AND DASHES

A dash is not a hyphen on steroids. These two marks have drastically different duties.

Hyphens punctuate words:

▶ They link prefixes and suffixes to root words. (*self-control, ex-president, globe-like*)

▶ They link smaller words to make compound words. (*go-between, powers-that-be, maids-of-honor*)

▶ They link related adjectives before nouns. (*high-impact logo, four-day seminar*)

Dashes, on the other hand, punctuate sentences. They make a detour from the main point of the sentence to an aside, an interrupter. If the interrupting comment comes in the middle of the sentence, use two of them—before and after the detour—like a set of parentheses.

If a hyphen is what you need (word punctuation), use this mark: -.

If a dash is what you need, here's the proper symbol—the mark here inside this sentence. Notice that a dash is twice as long as a hyphen and that there's no space before or after it. The words on both sides are flush left and right.

MEMORY TIP

Hyphenate words. Use dashes to punctuate sentences.

82

Dash Away, Dash Away, Dash Away All

DASHES VERSUS WELL-ORGANIZED SENTENCES

E-mails like the following example look like a brain dump, with the writer not having taken the time to sort main ideas from supporting detail. The reader has to do all the work.

Beulah Buchanan was in my office last week—she's the manager I mentioned who had experience as a project manager— and we discussed the big challenge brewing in Atlanta— whether you consider it a challenge or not, I certainly do. She and her staff are perfectly willing to allocate resources to help—they have several experienced specialists they can devote to the team—I think you met Tula, Weese, and Gertrude when you were here last month—they think they can find the financial contributors as well—that of course would be subject to senior management approval.

Organized:

Beulah Buchanan, the manager I mentioned who had experience as a project manager, was in my office last week. We discussed what I consider the big challenge brewing in Atlanta. She and her staff are perfectly willing to allocate resources to help, and they have several experienced specialists (Tula, Weese, and Gertrude, whom you met last month) they can devote to the team. They think they can find the financial contributors as well. Those contributors, of course, would be subject to senior management approval.

Dashes should never substitute for a well-organized sentence. Instead, they serve a good purpose: Dashes highlight what's between them or what follows them.

(Note: While we're on the subject of dashes, a question that pops up frequently in our grammar workshops is this: What's the difference between parentheses and dashes? Parentheses downplay what's inside them, while dashes do the opposite. Dashes highlight what follows or falls between them. In the above rewritten passage, parentheses around the names of the specialists downplay their names. Dashes around their names would highlight specifically who they are.)

MEMORY TIP

A little *dash* of dashes will do it. Sort the main ideas from the trivial so your reader doesn't have to.

83

No Death Knell for the Hyphen

HYPHENS BEFORE RELATED ADJECTIVES

You're walking along the sidewalk with friends, trying to select a restaurant for dinner in an unfamiliar city. Outside the door of one particular café, a sign says: "No smoking area available."

"How about this place for dinner?" your colleague asks.

"Won't work. Snuffy smokes. That sign says they don't have a smoking area available," you respond.

"I read it to mean just the opposite," your colleague argues and catches a waiter to clarify.

So which is it?

1. Is smoking not allowed anywhere in the restaurant?
2. Is smoking allowed, but the restaurant has an area for non-smokers?

The hyphen in such terms is missing so often that our eyes are trained to compensate for its absence. And for those who read literally and know from the context that such phrases could not be correct, the missing hyphen can cost a contract, halt a promotion, or end a relationship. For those who don't know the difference, they guess—with the same consequences.

Answer to the restaurant quandary:

No smoking area available. (With no hyphen, the sign means the entire restaurant is smoke-free. Snuffy cannot smoke there at all.)

No-smoking area available. (With this sign displayed, a restaurant allows smoking, but also has a smoke-free area.)

So what are a restaurant and a guy like Snuffy to do? Learn the four hyphen rules to avoid confusion:

▶ Hyphenate two related adjectives before a noun.

The boss attended a two-day workshop.

Kilpatrick advertises himself as a high-caliber motivational speaker.

We follow a 10-year cycle for equipment replacement.

Buy your over-the-counter medicines at a nearby pharmacy.

That station is known for up-to-the-minute reporting.

We navigated the snow-covered roads to the airport.

▶ Do not hyphenate related adjectives when they follow the noun (unless they are in altered or inverted form).

The workshop lasted two days.

Kilpatrick advertises himself as a motivational speaker of high caliber.

These medicines are available over the counter, without prescription.

Percival outlined his approach to investing in annuities that are tax-exempt. (inverted order—*tax-exempt annuities* is the typical order)

▶ Do not hyphenate related adjectives that precede a noun if the phrase is so well known that it's immediately recognizable and clear as a unit.

The rental car agency is liable for the damage.
The income tax form will be mailed to your home address.

▶ Do not hyphenate adverb-adjective combinations that precede a noun if the adverb ends in *–ly: selfishly arrogant, modestly rich, highly knowledgeable.*

Memory Tip

Related adjectives, like family members, work as a unit. So link them.

84

Matching Body Parts

CORRELATIVE LINKS

Like pie and ice cream, July 4th and parades, or the Super Bowl and parties, some words are always paired together: *either/or, neither/nor, not only/but also, if/whether.* When you use them together in the same sentence, make sure you link them properly.

Consider these pairs like handcuffs linking similar items together. Handcuffs link two equal hands. Likewise, you have to slap the "handcuffs" in front of two equivalent parts of a sentence: two nouns, two describing words (adjectives), two verbs, two clauses, and so forth. To do otherwise would be like handcuffing someone's left wrist to the right knee—more than a little awkward.

Incorrect:

We can *either* buy the house *or* the yacht with the inheritance.

Correct:

We can buy *either* the house *or* the yacht with the inheritance.

Incorrect:

Neither owns a Lexus *nor* a BMW.

Correct:

They own *neither* a Lexus *nor* a BMW.

Incorrect:

Not only is she intelligent, she's well liked.

Correct:

Not only is she intelligent, *but also* she's well liked.

MEMORY TIP

Visualize these links as handcuffs around matching "body parts" of the sentence skeleton.

85

Up a Tree Without a Paddle

MIXED METAPHORS

Similes and metaphors engage readers by comparing things in a memorable way: "The hailstorm on our new conference center sounded like a mortar attack." "Our sales force swarms the trade-show floor at every industry meeting, lighting at the elbow of every prospect attending." So far, so good. With these statements, we visualize the scene. Just be careful not to mix metaphors.

> If you work here, you have to learn to swim with the sharks, or you'll be taking enemy fire before you know it. (Are they swimming or fighting a war?)

> Our executives always want to run the ball themselves rather than pass it to staff. But if we're going to develop our managers, we need to set up a firewall and then permit them to make a few mistakes during their learning process. (Are they playing football or building a security system?)

Memory Tip

Rule 1 (in any sport): Keep your head in the game until the final whistle.

Rule 1 (with any comparison): Keep your metaphor in mind until you finish the thought.

86

As Much or More Than Most

PREPACKAGED COMPARISONS

Some comparisons come prepackaged at conception. The following list contains a few that probably roll off your tongue without much thought. Add a noun at the beginning and end of the comparison, and you have them wrapped up and ready to go—but a little jagged and ragged around the edges.

To see why each of these comparisons is "unequal" or incomplete, remove half the comparison and you'll notice the gap in logic.

One of the best: "Bruno is one of the best, if not the best, criminal lawyer in the state." Remove "if not the best" because that represents the second part of the comparison. Read what's left: "Bruno is one of the best criminal lawyer in the state." The writer is comparing Bruno to a group, but the group has been removed! Reword: "Bruno is one of the best criminal lawyers in the state, if not the best."

As bad or worse than: "The traffic in Houston is as bad or worse than in Chicago." Remove the second half of the comparison ("or worse than"), and you'll see what's missing here: "The traffic in Houston is as bad in Chicago." Reword: "The traffic in Houston is as bad as in Chicago, or worse."

As good or better than: "Brunhilda is as good or better than most managers about giving feedback." This is the same problem as with *as bad or worse than.* Reword: "Brunhilda is as good as most managers about giving feedback, or better."

As much or more than: "Eldora likes that country as much or more than most places where she does business." Again, the same issues surface. Remove the second part of the comparison ("or more than") to see what's incomplete: "Eldora likes that country as much most places where she does business." Reword: "Eldora likes that country as much as or more than any place where she does business."

When you're comparing two things, both ideas have to be complete.

MEMORY TIP

A comparison requires two groups or things—no shortcuts.

87

Doing the Splits

SPLIT INFINITIVES

An *infinitive* is the technical term for *to* plus a verb (an action word—what something does, has, or is). Examples: *to go, to eat, to report, to murder, to review, to seize, to manage, to be, to enjoy.*

Typically, it's taboo to tamper with these tidbits by putting words between the *to* and the action word if you can avoid it. Of course, if you have a good reason, such as to add emphasis, then go ahead and split the *to* from the verb. We'll let you be the judge of what you write—but English teachers everywhere are watching.

> To control this situation really, a supervisor must be at the plant site. (awkward)
> Really to control this situation, a supervisor must be at the plant site. (better)
> To *really* control this situation, a supervisor must be at the plant site. (adds emphasis)

> That approach will help you to effectively give employee feedback. (unnecessary split—a no-no)
> That approach will help you to give employee feedback effectively. (better)

Percival told me to periodically delay the project until our suppliers can catch up with shipments. (unnecessary split—a no-no)
Percival told me to delay the project periodically until our suppliers can catch up with shipments. (better)

When someone angrily yells, "Go to —," you probably know the
place they have in mind. But with infinitives, readers don't necessarily
know what's to follow. Hence, the suspense. Generally, you should finish the action before you let other words interrupt.

MEMORY TIP

As surely as two plus two equals four, *to* plus a verb equals one unit
of thought. Don't split it.

88

Without Just Cause

WITHOUT: WHAT IT CAN AND CAN'T DO

We build our highway systems much the way we build our sentences. Major interstates intersect with major highways, requiring elaborate overpasses, bridges, and on-and-off ramps. Minor roads also intersect with these same interstates, but they need less structured entrance and exit ramps.

Sentence construction follows the same logic; the links between the major and minor ideas match the roles they play. Words that link two major ideas are called *coordinating conjunctions*. Here's an all-inclusive list: *and, but, or, for, nor, so, yet.*

Words that link minor ideas to the major ones (the way minor roads join the major interstates) are called *subordinating conjunctions*. Here are a few: *if, although, until, because, unless, while, whether, after, before.*

A common mistake is to use *without* as a subordinating link (a conjunction).

Incorrect:

Kilpatrick could not get a promotion without he spent some time in Europe.

Orilla will flunk the test for a pilot's license without they change the criteria.

Without is *not* one of those bridges or linking words. It's a preposition, like *in, to, among, about, between, over, under,* and *by. Without* cannot link two clauses (groups of words with a subject and verb) in a sentence. Use *unless* instead as the proper link.

Correct:

> Kilpatrick could not get a promotion without spending some time in Europe. (correct because there's just one clause—*without* is a preposition here)
> Orilla will flunk the test for a pilot's license unless they change the criteria.

Incorrect:

> Fritz couldn't fly to Chicago without he asked his wife.

Correct:

> Fritz couldn't fly to Chicago until he asked his wife. (corrected by using a different link)

Incorrect:

> Ebeneezer cannot make a sale without he brags to everybody on the team.

Correct:

> Ebeneezer cannot make a sale without bragging to everybody on the team. (correct because there's just one clause—*without* is a preposition here)

MEMORY TIP

Without is without the power to link main ideas (clauses).

89

Getting Top Billing

PHRASAL PREPOSITIONS

Which of the following sentences is correct? Neither? Both?

> Pudge and Brunhilda have a ticket to fly to New York.
> Pudge as well as Brunhilda have a ticket to fly to New York.

If you chose only the first, you're correct. The verb in the second sentence should be *has* because *Pudge* is the guy we're primarily concerned about getting on the plane.

Consider the phrases *as well as*, *in addition to*, *together with*, and *along with* as afterthoughts and not part of a compound subject. (Technically, they're called *phrasal prepositions*, meanings prepositions of more than one word.) As an afterthought, they don't get equal ranking with the true subject of the sentence. So as my Italian friend from the Bronx would say, "fagettaboutem" when you select the verb.

These four phrases are *not* the equivalent of *and*. They do *not* make the noun that follows part of a compound subject. Examples:

Correct:

Gertrude and Tiger *are* on the board of directors.

Gertrude in addition to Tiger *is* on the board of directors. (Writers often set off such nonessential phrases with commas: "Gertrude, in addition to Tiger, is on the board of directors.")
Kilpatrick and his colleagues in Phoenix *have* been selected for the training. (Kilpatrick and the colleagues have equal status.)
Kilpatrick, as well as his colleagues in Phoenix, *has* been selected for the training. (The *as well as* phrase downplays *his colleagues*.)

So you may be asking, Why use one of those phrases to introduce the second noun? Why not just join the two nouns with *and*? Emphasis. *And* gives them equal status. The other phrases introduce a subordinate idea. If the noun or pronoun that follows them is not the main topic under discussion, keep them in their place!

▼

MEMORY TIP

Lean to the side, lower your voice, and whisper the aside beginning with *as well as, in addition to, along with,* or *together with* as if it were a secret. The correct verb for the true subject will become obvious.

90

A Branding Issue

CAPITALIZATION RULES FOR THE ROAD

To emphasize a word, you can bold it, italicize it, underline it, upper-case it, or change its font. But don't capitalize its initial letter. Capitalizing words randomly without a reason creates a grammar error. Capitalization signals the beginning of a new sentence or a proper noun (the specific name of a person, place, or thing—examples: Harvey Humpperdink, O'Hare Airport, Kleenex).

When applied improperly to random words, capitalization confuses readers and slows them down.

Basically, there's a simple way (analogy) and a more complex way (rules) to master capitalization. The simple analogy method will help you deal with most of the situations that surface.

Analogy Method:

Ask yourself if the term is a "brand name" or generic. If you're calling a noun by its brand name, capitalize it. If you're using its generic name, don't. Examples:

> The judge awarded the company $55,000 as a settlement.
> The judge awarded Adrico, Inc., $55,000 as a settlement.
> Are you driving a new car today?

Are you driving a new Chevrolet today?

Winnifred works in the building where our engineering group is located.

Winnifred works in Frazier Tower, where Engineering is located.

You need a requisition form to get shelving in your office.

You need Form 23HZ3 to get shelving in your office.

Rule Method:

For the few situations that this "brand name" analogy doesn't cover, here are the standard capitalization rules:

▶ Capitalize proper nouns, the names of specific places or regions. (Capitalize *city*, *state*, or *federal* only when the word is used as part of the actual name.)

the Dallas–Fort Worth Metroplex

Detroit

the Sabine River

the Tennessee Valley

the Northeast

Research Triangle

the Sahara Desert

the Antarctic

the Pacific Rim

▶ Capitalize races and languages.

Malay, Hindu, Russian, Finnish, Mandarin, Arabic, Spanish, Vietnamese, Egyptian

▶ Capitalize days of the week, months, and special days.

Tuesday, August, Christmas, Valentine's Day

▶ Capitalize historical periods and events.

the Great Depression, the Information Age

▶ Capitalize trade names, company names, organizations, divisions, and agencies.

Microsoft
Region 12 Auditing
Starbucks
Lexus Link
Homeland Security
The Salvation Army

▶ Capitalize the first word of a direct quotation (except when the quotation continues rather than begins a sentence).

The report states, "The project will end May 31."
"The project will end," according to this report, "by no later than May 31."

▶ Capitalize the first word, the last word, and all principal words in a heading or title.

Operating Costs for March (slide title)
The Exhaustion Cure: Up Your Energy from Low to Go in 21 Days (book title)
The Voice of Authority: 10 Communication Strategies Every Leader Needs to Know (book title)

Note: Occasionally, you'll find words such as *company*, *institution*, *bank*, *organization*, *employee*, or *buyer* capitalized in formal documents like policy statements or contracts. These common words have been substituted for the "brand names" after the complete name has been identified at the beginning of the document. For example, a real estate contract may identify "Mr. and Mrs. Bruno Trumpston, Sellers, and Dr. and Mrs. Diego Guiterrez, Buyers" at the beginning and then later refer only to *Sellers* and *Buyers* (capitalized to replace the specific names of the buyer and seller throughout the contract).

MEMORY TIP

Think "brand name" or generic. Capitalize accordingly.

91

Name, Rank, and Serial Number

Capitalization With Titles and Positions

Job titles trip people up and create havoc when they're used in a sentence. Technically, these still fit the "brand name" analogy mentioned in the last chapter. Ask yourself, is this person the only individual who will ever fill this position? If not, the usage is generic and deserves no capitalization.

Broaden your horizon from the standard few titles on a typical application form: *Mr.*, *Ms.*, *Mrs.*, and *Dr.* The range of titles runs the gamut from CEO to chief juggler: *Chairperson Bruno Bernstein, Dr. Bruno Bernstein, Director Bruno Bernstein, Maestro Bruno Bernstein, CEO Bruno Bernstein, Judge Bruno Bernstein, Vice President Bruno Bernstein.* If you're using the label as a title, it precedes the name and requires capitalization like any other ordinary title (*Mr.*, *Mrs.*, or *Dr.*).

If you're using the label only as a position and it follows the name, don't capitalize it:

He hired Orilla Ortega, vice president of finance, to take over in April. (a generic reference to the position she holds.)

Vice President of Finance Orilla Ortega will take over in April. (The title *Vice President of Finance* is used as a title before her name in lieu of *Dr.*, *Mrs.*, or *Ms.*)

Our new vice president of finance will take over in April. (a generic reference to the person without a name—not used as a title here.)

Our new vice president of finance, Orilla Ortega, will take over in April. (*Vice president of finance* is a generic reference to a position here; it is not used as a title because of the pronoun *our* and the commas around her name.)

Dr. Pudge Patel, chairman of the board, opposes the bill. (*Chairman* is a generic reference to the position he holds.)

Chairman of the Board Pudge Patel opposes the bill. (used as a title in front of the name, capitalized.)

Note: Here's an exception to the rule: Capitalize position titles of state, federal, or international officials of high distinction, such as President of the United States or cabinet members. *Mr. President.* *Madam Secretary.* Also keep in mind that some organizations create their own style rules, creating their own list of "high officials."

▼

MEMORY TIP

If the title precedes the name in lieu of a title such as Mr., Ms., or Dr., capitalize it. If it follows the name, don't.

92

Undercapitalized With No Regrets

THE CASE FOR LOWERCASE

Too much capitalization has the same effect as too much makeup, cologne, hair gel, or jewelry. It detracts, clutters and, in the case of grammar, confuses. Common words that are capitalized when they should not be typically fall into the following categories.

Random Words in Headings and Titles (Book Titles, Song Titles, Article Titles, Chapter Titles, Slide Titles)
You can blame your word-processing software for this error. I'm betting that your software automatically puts all words in "title case" or none in title case. It can't think and follow the real rules for capitalizing titles. Here they are:

▶ Capitalize the first, the last, and all principal words in headings and titles.

▶ Unless they are the first or last words in a line, do not capitalize prepositions of three letters or fewer (*by, for, in, at, to, on*), conjunctions (*and, but, or, nor, so, yet*), or the articles *a, an, the.*

A common goof occurs when someone considers a long word to be a "principal" word and, conversely, considers a short word to be a minor word. Length has no more to do with the importance of words than height has to do with the importance of people.

To capitalize correctly, you have to recognize the part of speech (preposition, conjunction, verb, and so forth).

Incorrect:

Sales Volume is Growing in New Regions (*Is* is a principal word. It is part of the verb of the entire sentence!)

Correct:

Sales Volume Is Growing in New Regions

Incorrect:

Suggestions By Teams At Corporate And Field Offices

Correct:

Suggestions by Teams at Corporate and Field Offices

The Words *Federal, State, City*

Our city officials hired him as sheriff, and then he worked out of state for several years, finally returning to work for the federal government in several positions before his death.

The Names of Seasons

She takes a sabbatical in the spring.

The Terms for Directions

He moved further northwest with his job after his parents died.

Turn south toward the corporate headquarters.

But: The South typically votes Democratic on such issues. (a region)

MEMORY TIP

This sentence will remind you of the categories of things not to capitalize: "There should be a *law* (laws have titles) against *driving* (directions) *downtown* (federal, state, or city government offices) in *summer* (seasons)."

PART 10

Misspelled and Misused Words

Use this last section as a checklist for frequent review. I compiled and published a similar list of frequently misspelled and misused words years ago when our company began leading writing and grammar workshops, and I have been adding to it ever since.

Feel free to send your personal favorites to me at mailroom @booher.com, and I'll get them into either our Communication Tip of the Month (sign up at www.booher.com) or my blog (Communicate With Confidence at www.Booher.com/BooherBanter).

Or, if you haven't already done so before beginning this book, you may want to assess your mastery of some of these with our free online assessment (www.BooherRules.com).

Let's tackle these last few traps.

93

Would You Spell That for Me?

FREQUENTLY MISSPELLED WORDS

Mark Twain once said of the U.S. copyright laws: "Whenever the copyright law is to be made or altered, then the idiots assemble." The same could be said about English spelling.

Of course, we didn't have a Czar of Spelling at any particular time in our history to dictate our spelling rules; instead, English has incorporated words from many other languages. That's the reason for the current spelling mess and why we have, for example, several ways to spell the same sound: *fun, fluff, phone, enough.*

The most common spelling errors stem from these questions:

Does that word end in *–ible* or *–able?*
Is there a double *n* or just one? Just one *t* or two?
Should that be *–ei* or *–ie?*
Which *–ceed* is that—*ceed? cede? sede?*

Enough whining. The following list includes the most commonly misspelled words. As you review these, either memorize them or relate them to the rules following the list. Just don't give up and jump out an 87th-floor window.

accessible	beneficial
accommodate	boulevard
accumulate	bulletin
accurate	buoyant
achieve	calendar
acknowledgment	camouflage
admittance	category
adolescent	cellar
allege	cemetery
allotted	changeable
analyze	choose
anonymous	chose
antiquated	colossal
apparatus	commitment
apparent	committed
appearance	competent
argument	complexion
ascertain	comptroller
bankruptcy	conceivable
beginning	conscience

conscientious	enthusiastically
consciousness	etiquette
consensus	exceed
controversy	excel
definite	exhibition
dependent	existence
depreciation	exorbitant
describe	extension
description	facilitate
detrimental	familiar
diligence	feasible
discrepancy	forty
discrimination	fraudulent
dilemma	fulfill
disappoint	gauge
dissipate	grammar
efficiency	grievance
embarrass	harass
endeavor	hereditary
enforceable	hindrance

humorous	irresistible
hygiene	itinerary
hypocrisy	knowledgeable
imitate	legitimate
imperative	liable
implement	license
inadvertent	likelihood
incidentally	livelihood
indefinite	loose
independent	lose
indispensable	luxurious
inflationary	magnificent
ingenious	magnificence
initial	maintenance
initiative	manageable
innate	maneuver
innocent	martyr
insistent	mechanics
interference	mileage
irrelevant	miniature

miscellaneous	personnel
mischievous	perspiration
municipal	phenomenon
naïve	pneumonia
necessary	precede
negligible	preferred
ninety	prestige
noticeable	prevalent
occasionally	privilege
occurred	probably
occurrence	procedure
overrated	proceed
pamphlet	proportion
parallel	psychoanalyze
pastime	quandary
perform	questionnaire
permanent	quietly
permissible	quit
perseverance	quite
persistent	recede

receive	synonymous
recommend	technician
reconciliation	technique
recurrence	tendency
reference	tragedy
referred	transcend
reminiscence	transmittal
repetition	transparent
seize	twelfth
separate	unanimous
siege	undoubtedly
sieve	unscrupulous
similar	vacuum
souvenir	vengeance
stopped	ventilation
succeed	versatile
succession	vigilance
superfluous	waive
superintendent	warranty
supersede	whether

wholly	withhold

Misspelled words generally fall into these categories: (1) those caused by the *ei* versus *ie* dilemma, (2) double consonants, or (3) adding the suffix *–ible* or *–able*.

EI Rules:
▶ Use *–i* before *–e*, except after *–c*, to make the long *–e* sound (*achieve, relieve, believe*). The five exceptions to this rule can be summed up in this sentence: "It's *weird* that *neither* of us *seized* this rule and learned it *either* at school or at *leisure*."
▶ Use *–e* before *–i* after *–c* to make the long *–e* sound (*receive, deceive, receipt*).
▶ Use *–e* before *–i* when the sound is *not* a long *–e* (*eight, weight, neighbor*).

Suffixes *–able* and *–ible*:
Adding these suffixes to verbs and nouns forms adjectives. The spelling problem involves knowing whether to add *–ible* or *–able* because they have generally the same meaning: "capable of being."

justify + able = justifiable
quote + able = quotable
repair + able = repairable
do + able = doable
verify + able = verifiable
response + ible = responsible

permission + ible = permissible

As a general rule, you can determine the correct spelling by considering related words. Do they end in *–ation*? If so, use *–able*. If the related word ends in *–ion* or *–ive*, then use *–ible*.

reprehensive	reprehensible
responsive	responsible
justification	justifiable
quotation	quotable
extension	extensible

Prefixes

Very few prefixes still require hyphenation: *all-*, *self-*, *ex-*, and occasionally *anti-*. That's it.

all-	all-around
ex-	ex-president
self-	self-conscious
anti-	anti-inflammatory (but antibiotic)

Write all the remaining prefixes solid with the root words:

non-	nonessential
intra-	intramural
inter-	interstate
un-	uninvolved
im	immobilized
contra-	contrariwise
mis-	mishandled
semi-	semiautomatic
sub-	substantiate

pseudo-	pseudointellectual
pre-	pretest
post-	posthumously
re-	reupholster
half-	halfhearted
over-	overestimate
under-	undercapitalized

Note two exceptions to the above list:

1. Use a hyphen when the root word is a proper noun or adjective (*un-American, pro-Democracy, mid-April, pre-Elizabethan*).
2. Use a hyphen when its omission would cause misreading. (Recover versus recover: "He kept trying to re-cover the merchandise on the truck because of the forecasted hailstorm." Or: "He kept trying to recover the stolen truck." Re-count versus recount: "They insisted we re-count the votes." Or: "He wanted to recount the whole story of the accident." Re-sort versus resort: "They should re-sort these brochures." Or: "I made our reservations at a five-star resort.")

Suffixes

Suffixes are added to the end of a word. Sometimes the spelling of the word changes, and sometimes it doesn't. There are too many categories and exceptions to make memorization of suffix "rules" helpful. But it is helpful to know that only one suffix always requires a hyphen: *–elect*.

foursome
restless
carefully
counterclockwise

squeamish
wholesomeness
sphere-like (but *childlike* doesn't require a hyphen)
chairman-elect (always requires a hyphen)

MEMORY TIP

For the *–ceed/–cede/–sede* sound: The only word that ends in *–sede* is *supersede*. Only three words end in *–ceed*. You can remember them all with this sentence: *If you want to succeed in life, proceed to exceed.* All other words with this sound are spelled with the *–cede* ending.

For the *ei* dilemma: Remember this little ditty: "You'll get salt in your eyes (*I's*) if they get too close to the seas (*C's*)."

94

May I See Your References, Please?

SPELLING RULES FOR PLURAL FORMS

Making nouns plural creates other spelling hazards. (You knew things couldn't be that simple, right?) Let's go from easy to more difficult here with the rules:

▶ *Regular nouns:* Add an –s.

idea	ideas
desk	desks
driveway	driveways
freedom	freedoms
building	buildings
client	clients

▶ *Irregular nouns:* Memorize these. (You've probably learned these intuitively as different words. Their spellings may change internally or may not change at all from the singular to the plural form.)

mouse	mice
foot	feet
child	children

woman	women
sheep	sheep
species	species
deer	deer
headquarters	headquarters
measles	measles
physics	physics
mathematics	mathematics
news	news

▶ *Nouns ending in* –s, –ss, –z, –sh, –ch, *and* –x: Add –es.

fox	foxes
box	boxes
watch	watches
crutch	crutches
lunch	lunches
brush	brushes
bush	bushes
loss	losses
toss	tosses
buzz	buzzes

▶ *Nouns ending in* –f *or* –fe: Add –s *to some. For others, change* –f *to* –v *and add* –es.

shelf	shelves
half	halves
scarf	scarves
life	lives
wife	wives
café	cafés
carafe	carafes
cuff	cuffs

▶ *Nouns ending in –y preceded by a consonant:* Change –y to –i and add –es.

city	cities
county	counties
category	categories
secretary	secretaries
worry	worries

▶ *Nouns ending in –y preceded by a vowel:* Add –s.

attorney	attorneys
valley	valleys
holiday	holidays
delay	delays

▶ *Nouns ending in –o:* Add –s or –es. (But: all musical and literary terms ending in –o add –s to form their plurals.)

potato	potatoes
hero	heroes
zero	zeroes
portfolio	portfolios
studio	studios
piano	pianos
soprano	sopranos

▶ *Compound words written as two words or hyphenated:* Make the primary word plural. If there is no primary word, add –s to the end of the compound.

commander in chief	commanders in chief
mother-in-law	mothers-in-law
secretary of state	secretaries of state
account receivable	accounts receivable
bill of lading	bills of lading
rule of thumb	rules of thumb

maid of honor	maids of honor
look-alike	look-alikes
stand-in	stand-ins
go-between	go-betweens
die-hard	die-hards
ne'er-do-well	ne'er-do-wells

▶ *Foreign words:* Some words retain the plural from their original language. With others, their plurals now conform to English rules.

Singular	Plural
alumnus	alumni
chassis	chassis
plateau	plateaus
datum	data
prognosis	prognoses
synopsis	synopses
crisis	crises
ellipsis	ellipses
hypothesis	hypotheses
thesis	theses
addendum	addenda

But:

Singular	Foreign Plural	English Plural
appendix	appendices	appendixes
index	indices	indexes
candelabrum	candelabra	candelabrums
tempo	tempi	tempos
criterion	criteria	criteria

forum	fora	forums
cranium	crania	craniums
crux	cruces	cruxes
matrix	matrices	matrixes

MEMORY TIP

Latch onto a few examples and extrapolate the rules. Or, check a good online dictionary.

95

Messing With My Head

HYPHENATE? SOLID? TWO WORDS?

"Why don't you follow up with me after the meeting?" Do you need a hyphen in the previous sentence? "The manager read the follow-up report and grew livid." How about the hyphen in the previous sentence? Both are correct—with and without the hyphens. How can that be possible?

Actors play many roles during their careers. In one movie, an actor may be an astronaut exploring the unknown in a spacesuit. In another, he's a pistol-toting bank robber. In still another, he's sacrificed millions to don a monk's robe.

Similarly, words play different roles in a sentence. If hyphenation confuses you, maybe it's not the words themselves but the roles they play in a particular sentence that create the problem. Just as actors dress "in character," here are the rules of the varying roles for words:

▶ Nouns are written as either a solid or a hyphenated compound.
▶ Verbs are written as two words.
▶ Two related adjectives before a noun are hyphenated.

Correct:
Pongo asked for client *follow-up* after the meeting. (noun)

Pongo will *follow up* with the client after the meeting. (verb)
Pongo gave me a *follow-up* report after the meeting. (adjective)

Give me a *breakdown* on the cost. (noun)
Please *break down* the costs for travel by individual. (verb)
The *break-down* instructions for the trade-show booth are sketchy.
    (adjective)

The *step-up* in royalty payments is only 2 percent. (noun)
Why don't you *step up* your efforts to close the deal. (verb)
The *step-up* plan for payment seems reasonable. (adjective)

MEMORY TIP

Think of the movies: Ask yourself what role the words play in the sentence. Then hyphenate accordingly.

96

I Resemble That Remark

AFFECT VERSUS EFFECT

You can't depend on your spell-checker to make final decisions when it highlights suspicious words. For example, neither of the following sentences has a misspelled word; they both are correct but have different meanings.

> The law before Congress will effect a widespread change in small businesses. (*effect: –*to cause)
> The law before Congress will affect a widespread change in small businesses. (*affect: –*to involve or influence)

The choice between the two can be enormous.

The most common mistake, however, with these two words—and a usage that's always wrong—is this: *Affect* is never a noun. (Note: The one exception to the broad generalization I just made is that *affect* is a noun, a technical term, in the specialized fields of psychiatry or psychology. But don't let that one exception keep you from latching onto this otherwise very helpful memory aid.)

Incorrect:

> I work for an inspiring manager, and she has a big affect on how well I do my job.

Correct:

> I work for an inspiring manager, and she has a big effect on how well I do my job. (influence)

Here's a rule of thumb that will help you keep these two words straight about 90 percent of the time:

▶ When you need a noun, typically you need *effect*. (Occasionally, it's a verb.)

▶ When you need a verb, you need *affect*.

The tricky part is the other 10 percent of the time: *Effect* can be both a noun and a verb. As a verb, it means "to cause." As a noun, it means "a cause" or "a result."

Examples with Effect (noun: a result or a cause):

> The effect of his decision will be devastating.
>
> I'm not sure what effect his transfer will have on the new managers.
>
> The effects of the heavy wind were evident to our factory visitors.

Examples with Effect (verb: to cause):

> Merit raises of 15 percent will effect a boost in morale.
>
> A downsizing always effects massive change in a company's culture.
>
> The roll-ups of several small companies have effected an industry upheaval unlike anything we've seen in the past three decades.

Examples with Affect (verb: to influence or involve):

> That policy affects my paycheck.
>
> His decision affects my career.
>
> The weather affects the distribution of our product.

MEMORY TIP

Affect starts with –*a*; it's an action word—the verb. *Affect* can never be a noun (exception: in psychiatry).

The *effect* (result) of learning the difference between the two words will positively *affect* (influence) your career.

97

Do I Have Your Guarantee?

ENSURE, INSURE, ASSURE?

The synonyms *ensure*, *assure*, and *insure* mean to give a guarantee. Synonyms can replace each other in some contexts—but not in all. For example, *big, large, huge, gigantic,* and *enormous* are synonyms. But these words can't always be used interchangeably. I might say, "Hortense gave a *big* speech to all the employees last week about cutting expenses." But I wouldn't say, "Hortense gave an *enormous* speech to all employees last week about cutting expenses."

Synonyms are similar, but they're not interchangeable in all contexts. So back to *ensure, assure,* and *insure.*

Ensure (to guarantee or make certain—use in cases other than when referring to people):
This new packaging will ensure that the product arrives safely.

Insure (to make certain or protect against loss—use when referring to monetary payments):
This bond will insure payment up to $2,000.

Assure (to pledge or give confidence to people—use in the same way as reassure):

He assured us that he would attend.

Her e-mail assured the customer that our report would be submitted before the deadline.

MEMORY TIP

Insure: Insurance companies spell their names with an *–i*. They make monetary payments. Use the *–i* word when talking about money.

Assure: People reassure you. Use the *–a* word when talking about people giving assurances.

Ensure: Use the *–e* word in all other situations.

98

It's a Matter of Principle

PRINCIPLE VERSUS PRINCIPAL

The confusion between these words occurs because *principal* can be both a noun and an adjective. But because business professionals are much more familiar with the noun form ("Orilla, a principal in the law firm of Humperdink, Vanderslink, and Hoodwink . . ."), when they need an adjective, they select the opposite word.

Wrong! Wrong! Wrong! Stay with the correct word *principal* (meaning *primary*, *chief*, or *main*), understanding that it can be both an adjective and a noun.

Principal (adjective: chief, primary, main):
Our principal product is running shoes.

Principal (noun: one who has control):
Trudy Trott, a principal in our accounting firm, works in the New York office.

Principle (noun: a rule or guideline):
Our organization operates by this general principle: Customers are reasonable.

MEMORY TIP

A principal way to remember principles is to post them on placards.

99

A Good Example

E.G. VERSUS *I.E.*

The meanings of these two Latin abbreviations are commonly reversed. Unless you're learning to speak the dead language Latin, when you see these abbreviations, substitute the English equivalent and there'll be no confusion.

e.g. (stands for the Latin phrase *exempli gratia*, meaning *for example*)
> He takes far too many supplements, e.g., vitamins, iron, calcium, beta-carotene, sleep-aid tablets, and diuretics.

i.e. (stands for the Latin phrase *id est*, meaning *that is*)
> He believes in reincarnation, i.e., a second life possibly as a tree.

Reminder: Both phrases require a comma before and after them.

MEMORY TIP

Both *e.g.* and *example* begin with the letter *e*.

100

How Are You?

NAUSEATED VERSUS NAUSEOUS

This pair of troublesome words slipped into the book above other difficult pairs for several reasons. People seeking *advice* on how best to *advise* people about improving their language and writing skills can call *disinterested* parties for help. (Those troublesome words are actually easy: *Advice* is a noun, while *advise* is a verb.) *Disinterested* parties are those objective, impartial people willing to help, while uninterested parties are those who aren't willing to give them the time of day.

The *nauseated/nauseous* pair also beat out others in the crunch for space for this reason: Our consultants frequently *counsel* clients by phone on such matters. In fact, your own organization may have a Grammar *Council* set up in corporate headquarters for this very purpose. I'm sure they're *discreet* in pointing out errors so that no one is embarrassed to ask for document reviews. In fact, they may even be able to set up *discrete* funds (separate, distinct from the total) for each individual employee to pay for outside writing training. They could *disburse* these funds when employees meet certain criteria. (Good intentions are often *dispersed* to the wind, however, and these learning opportunities are never followed up in a formal way.)

But I digress about my decision. Back to the point: Considering space limitations and your options for gaining knowledge on other confusing twosomes, this chapter focuses on the commonly confused pair *nauseated/nauseous*.

Incorrect:
I'm not going to do the presentation because I'm feeling nauseous.

Correct:
I'm not going to do the presentation because I'm feeling nauseated.

Nauseated (adjective: sick):
Our CEO becomes nauseated before each board meeting.

Nauseous (adjective: sickening):
The smell of coffee is nauseous to me.

Memory Tip

Nauseated contains "seated" within it. When you feel nauseated, you should be seated.

101

Is Success Imminent?

EMINENT VERSUS IMMINENT

Certainly your career success is imminent—just as soon as you master these last two words.

Eminent (adjective: outstanding, prominent):
Franz is an eminent leader in the community because of his charitable work.

Imminent (adjective: impending; about to happen):
According to all the rumors, your winning the promotion is imminent!

MEMORY TIP

Link these pairs of ideas with the initial letters of each word:

eminent and evident (prominent, outstanding)
imminent and immediate (about to happen)

Bibliography

Booher, Dianna. *E-Writing: 21st-Century Tools for Effective Communication.* New York: Simon & Schuster/Pocket Books, 2001.

_____. *Good Grief, Good Grammar: The Business Person's Guide to Grammar and Usage.* Ballantine Books, Canada, 1988.

Lederer, Richard, and John Shore. *Comma Sense: A Fundamental Guide to Punctuation.* New York: St. Martin's Press, 2005.

Strunk, William Jr., and E. B. White. *The Elements of Style,* 4th ed. New York: Longman, 1999.

American Heritage Dictionary of the English Language, 4th ed. Boston: Houghton Mifflin, 2000.

Chicago Manual of Style, 15th ed. Chicago: University of Chicago Press, 2003.

New Oxford American Dictionary, 2nd ed. New York: Oxford University Press, 2005.

Resources by Dianna Booher Available from Booher Consultants

Books: Selected Titles

Good Grief, Good Grammar

E-Writing: 21st Century Tools for Effective Communication

Speak with Confidence: Powerful Presentations That Inform, Inspire and Persuade

Communicate with Confidence: How to Say It Right the First Time and Every Time

From Contact to Contract: 496 Proven Sales Tips to Generate More Leads, Close More Deals, Exceed Your Goals, and Make More Money

Great Personal Letters for Busy People

Executive's Portfolio of Model Speeches for All Occasions

Winning Sales Letters

To the Letter: A Handbook of Model Letters for the Busy Executive

The Complete Letterwriter's Almanac

Clean Up Your Act: Effective Ways to Organize Paperwork and Get It Out of Your Life

The New Secretary: How to Handle People as Well as You Handle Paper

Writing for Technical Professionals

First Thing Monday Morning

Get a Life Without Sacrificing Your Career
Get Ahead, Stay Ahead
Ten Smart Moves for Women
The Esther Effect
The Worth of a Woman's Words
Well Connected: Power Your Own Soul by Plugging Into Others
Your Signature Work: Creating Excellence and Influencing Others at Work
Your Signature Life: Pursuing God's Best Every Day
Fresh-Cut Flowers for a Friend
Love Notes: From My Heart to Yours
Mother's Gifts to Me
The Little Book of Big Questions: Answers to Life's Perplexing Questions

Workshops
Strategic Writing™
Email Matters™
Technical Writing
Developing Winning Proposals
Good Grief, Good Grammar
eService Communications
Communicate with Confidence®
Customer Service Communications
Presentations That Work®
Listening until You Really Hear
Resolving Conflict
Meetings: Leading and Participating Productively™
Negotiating so that Everyone Wins

For More Information

For more information, please contact:

Booher Consultants, Inc.
2051 Hughes Rd.
Grapevine, TX 76051
Phone: (817) 318-6000
E-mail: mailroom@booher.com
Web site: www.booher.com and www.DiannaBooher.com
E-store: www.BooherDirect.com
Dianna's blog: www.booher.com/booherbanter
Assessment: BooherRules.com

For more grammar and writing tips (plus tips on presentations and interpersonal skills), subscribe to our complimentary *Communication Tip of the Month* at www.Booher.com.

Take our online grammar assessment at www.BooherRules.com.

Index

About the Author

Dianna Booher works with organizations to increase their productivity and improve their effectiveness through better communication: oral, written, interpersonal, and cross-functional.

As an internationally recognized business communication expert, she is the author of 44 books published in 31 foreign editions, as well as numerous videos, audio CDs, and Web-based e-learning products for improving communication and productivity. She is the founder and president of Booher Consultants, a communication training firm based in the Dallas/Fort Worth Metroplex. The company's programs target all forms of corporate communication:

- ▶ Written documents (e-mail, proposals, reports, letters, procedures)
- ▶ Oral presentations to management and sales presentations to clients
- ▶ Meetings
- ▶ One-on-one interactions with colleagues, strategic partners, and customers

Booher's approach to corporate and personal effectiveness focuses on the essential business communication skills that have universal application and are necessary for success in any industry or profession.

The firm provides communication consulting and training to some of the largest Fortune 500 companies and government agencies, among them Lockheed Martin, Marriott, Siemens, Alcatel-Lucent, USAA, Bank of America, Hyatt, Merrill Lynch, Principal Financial, Northwestern Mutual, JPMorgan Chase, PepsiCo, Frito-Lay, Bayer, Nokia, JCPenney, the Army and Air Force Exchange Service, U.S. Department of Veterans Affairs, and NASA.

Successful Meetings magazine has recognized Dianna in its list of "21 Top Speakers for the 21st Century." *Executive Excellence Publishing* has named her to its list of "Top 100 Minds on Personal Development" and "Top 100 Thought Leaders in America." She has also won the highest awards in her industry, having been inducted into the National Speakers Association's Speaker Hall of Fame. Dianna earned a master's degree in English from the University of Houston.

For more information about bringing the Booher team into your organization to help you meet your own communication challenges, visit www.booher.com, or call (800) 342-6621.